BALDRIGE
ON
CAMPUS

BALDRIGE ON CAMPUS

The Assessment Workbook for Higher Education

Donald C. Fisher

QUALITY RESOURCES.
A Division of The Kraus Organization Limited

Most Quality Resources books are available at quantity discounts when purchased in bulk. For more information contact:

Special Sales Department
Quality Resources
A Division of The Kraus Organization Limited
902 Broadway
New York, New York 10010
800-247-8519

Printed in the United States of America

97 96 95   10 9 8 7 6 5 4 3 2 1

Quality Resources
A Division of the Kraus Organization Limited
902 Broadway
New York, New York 10010
800-247-8519

The paper used in this publication meets the minimum requirements of American National Standard for Information Sciences--Permanence of Paper for Printed Library Materials, ANSI Z39.48-1984.

ISBN: 0-527-76298-9

Library of Congress Cataloging-in-Publication Data

Fisher, Donald C.
    Baldrige on campus : the assessment workbook for higher education
Donald C. Fisher.
        p.   cm.
    Includes Bibliographical references (p.   ).
    ISBN 0-527-76298-9 (alk. paper)
    1. Education, Higher—United States—Administraton—Handbooks,
manuals, etc.   2. Universities and colleges—United States-
-Evaluation—Handbooks, Manuals, etc.   3. Total quality management-
-United States—Handbooks, manuals, etc.   I. Title.
LB2341.f493   1995
    378.1'07—dc20   95-17317
                                                            C I P

To my mother

Robbie Cruse Fisher

for working long hours
to help support four children's
college educations

and

To my mother-in-law

Murrell Madrey

for her lifelong
love for education

CONTENTS_____

FOREWORD————————————

In 1992, the National Institute of Standards and Technology, who oversee the Baldrige Award, began to examine the applicability and utility of the award for educational institutions. The examination included networking with educators, educational associations, institutions who were actively pursuing excellence through quality improvement methods, and their business partners. The consensus of the groups was that the Baldrige Criteria would allow a framework for assessing the level and extent of quality efforts on campus along dimensions important to educational excellence and provide a template for planning strategic directions for improvements.

The Baldrige Education Criteria maintain the same seven category framework as the Business Criteria. The modifications in structure and items to address are designed to accommodate the central mission of educational organizations to provide a well-educated workforce and citizenry. Maintaining student success and institutional effectiveness as the central focus of the Criteria separates the Baldrige institutional assessment from other assessments.

Dr. Fisher's book provides institutions with a method for conducting a self-assessment using the Baldrige Education Criteria and a consistent scoring system for analyzing the information gathered to generate strategic plans for improvement. The resulting report can serve as a baseline of current activity, a guide to future action, and an accumulation of data that can be accessed for more formal reports to be used in accreditation, application for such awards as the National Association of College and University Business Officers' (NACUBO) Innovative Management Award, the Baldrige Award, and others.

Dr. Fisher has served as an educator, a development officer for a major company, and chief executive of a quality center that is a joint project of a college and large metropolitan chamber of commerce. His experiences as a Baldrige examiner, a President's Award examiner, a senior judge for the Secretary of the Air Force Quality Award, and a judge for the Tennessee Quality Award and Greater Memphis Area Award afford him a unique perspective in the examination of quality in an educational setting. Diligent use of this book should generate the type of information that can be used to accelerate improvement efforts, allowing increased student and stakeholder satisfaction and enhanced institutional effectiveness.

Linda G. James
Systems Management Consultant
University of Tennessee at Martin

former Education Specialist
Malcolm Baldrige National Quality Award

PREFACE _____

This workbook has been written as a result of the author's involvement in helping develop the National Association of College and University Business Officers (NACUBO) Innovative Management Achievement Awards (IMAA) program. The purpose of this program is to recognize college and university achievements in improving quality and reducing the cost of higher education programs and services. While the IMAA program was specifically developed by NACUBO to evaluate management effectiveness and innovation in higher education, the IMAA evaluation criteria are modeled after the Malcolm Baldrige National Quality Award Criteria for Education.

In 1993 NACUBO teamed with Barnes & Noble Bookstores, Inc. to develop the IMAA Award and to begin a long-term sponsorship in which Barnes & Noble provide an annual financial contribution to the program and assist in management support and program publicity efforts.

This workbook was developed out of the NACUBO and Barnes & Noble project and is based upon the Malcolm Baldrige National Quality Award Criteria for Education, which sets a standard of excellence for institutions seeking the highest levels of overall quality performance and service delivery. The award process encompasses broad-based or institution-wide student and management programs designed to improve or enhance service quality, streamline administrative structures, and/or significantly reduce costs and cycle-time in the areas of academic affairs, student services, and business/finance. This Baldrige assessment workbook is designed to help faculty and staff assess their institution's total quality initiatives. It will also help those interested in writing a comprehensive award application.

The Baldrige Award Criteria for Education addresses all key requirements for institutions to achieve quality excellence and student focus. The Criteria focus not only on institutional results, but also on the conditions and processes that lead to those results. Thus, this assessment workbook offers a framework that institutions can use to tailor their systems and processes toward ever-higher quality performance and student focus.

A pilot assessment using this workbook was conducted at the State Technical Institute at Memphis, a two-year college located in Memphis, Tennessee. Twenty-two faculty, staff, and senior administrators attended a two-day workshop learning how to use the workbook and prepare for a campus-wide assessment. In addition to attendees from the host institution, representatives from the University of Tennessee at Knoxville and Martin, and the U. S. Air Force Quality Institute at Maxwell Air Force Base, Montgomery, Alabama, were represented. The entire team consisted of vice-presidents, deans, department heads, faculty, and staff from all the institutions represented.

The assessment training was conducted by the author and Linda James who served as chief administrator of the national project to rewrite the Baldrige Criteria for Education for the Malcolm Baldrige National Quality Award program in Gaithersburg, Maryland.

In addition, a second pilot using this workbook was conducted at the University of Tennessee at Martin. Several faculty, staff, and various levels of administrators attended the two-day workshop. University assessment teams used the workbook to conduct a campus-wide assessment. Findings from both pilot assessments have been incorporated into workbook improvements.

I want to thank Linda James for her review of all the Baldrige Criteria questions that were simplified and rewritten with zero-based and world-class examples. This was a phenomenal task.

In addition, I would like to thank Captain Mark Danis, of the U. S. Air Force Quality Institute, who has provided his expertise in reviewing this workbook for content and strategic usefulness. His review prompted the author to add chapter ten, which helps transform the workbook assessment findings into actionable strategies.

INTRODUCTION _____

This Baldrige assessment workbook will become an invaluable tool to use to better understand the Baldrige Criteria. In this workbook the compounded Baldrige Criteria questions have been rewritten for institutions of higher education and simplified for easier understanding. Institutions can use this workbook as a guide for self-assessment and strategic planning. Another use of the workbook is for collecting data to ultimately write a quality award application.

The Malcolm Baldrige National Quality Award Education Criteria are directed toward delivering improved value to students and stakeholders while simultaneously maximizing the overall effectiveness of the institution. The Baldrige Criteria are built around seven major examination categories:

EXAMINATION CATEGORIES[1]

CATEGORY 1

Leadership: The senior institutional officers' success in creating and sustaining a quality culture.

- Senior institutional officers develop goals and operational plans to achieve total quality leadership and management.

- Senior institutional leaders promote student success and institutional effectiveness.

- Institutional leaders initiate, develop, and encourage partnerships with students, faculty, staff, administration, boards of directors, community agencies, government, civic organizations, business, industry, and suppliers to the institution.

---

[1] Source: 1995 Education Pilot Criteria, Malcolm Baldrige National Quality Award.

CATEGORY 2

Information and Analysis: The effectiveness of information collection and data analysis to support the overall mission-related performance of the institution.

- The quality initiative is reflected and integrated through the institution's use of data analysis and information to support its overall mission.

- Educational institutions base all quality initiatives on facts and data.

- A quality information system requires consistency and linkages among the components of the system through integrated, consistent, and understandable communication institution-wide.

CATEGORY 3

Strategic and Operational Planning: The effectiveness of systems and processes for assuring the quality of programs and services.

- Faculty, staff, suppliers, students, and stakeholders receiving services provided by educational institutions are involved in the institution's planning process.

- Strategic and operational planning is an annual process focused on continuous improvement.

- All institutional planning is focused on serving students better.

CATEGORY 4

Human Resource Development and Management: The success of efforts to realize the full potential of the work force to meet the institution's quality and performance objectives.

- Educational institutions create a work force that recognizes and utilizes diversity of faculty, staff, and students.

- Problem-solving tools and techniques are taught to the work force to help them reduce and eliminate reoccurring problems and process upsets.

- Educational institutions train and develop the work force on a continuous basis.

CATEGORY 5

Education and Business Process Management: The effectiveness of systems and processes for assuring the quality of programs and services.

- Educational institutions are focused toward process improvement and cycle-time reduction.

- Continuous improvement is part of the management of all systems and processes throughout the institution.

- Educational institutions focus on well-designed and well-executed systems and processes.

CATEGORY 6

Institution's Performance Results: The improvement of student and operational performance, demonstrated through qualitative measures.

- Educational institutions measure and monitor student achievement and institutional process improvement on a continuous basis.

- Educational institutions document and share trend data throughout the institution. Trend data demonstrate progress over a period of time and show that improvements are sustained.

- Educational institutions measure supplier involvement and ensure that ongoing improvement is being addressed.

CATEGORY 7

Satisfaction of Those Receiving Services: The effectiveness of systems to determine student and stakeholder requirements and demonstrated success in meeting them.

- Quality is defined as meeting student needs and stakeholder requirements. Each institution defines its stakeholders. They may include students, the community, society, colleges and universities, and business and/or industry.

- The senior leadership of an educational institution creates and sustains a student and stakeholder focus and clear and visible quality values for the different students and stakeholders both within and outside the institution.

- The institution is student focused and determines user satisfaction through surveys and focus groups.

The Baldrige Award

BACKGROUND

The Malcolm Baldrige National Quality Award program was established in 1987 and named in honor of the former secretary of commerce under President Ronald Reagan.

The Baldrige program establishes guidelines and criteria that can be used by organizations in evaluating their own quality improvement efforts. The Malcolm Baldrige National Quality Award encourages quality improvement throughout all sectors of the economy. The secretary of commerce and the National Institute of Standards and Technology are given responsibilities to develop and manage the award with cooperation and financial support from the private sector.

Award recipients are expected to share information about successful quality strategies with other organizations. The award is traditionally presented annually by the president of the United States and the secretary of commerce at special ceremonies in Washington, D.C. During 1995, pilot criteria for health care and education were derived from the Baldrige Award Business Criteria.[2]

Baldrige Goes for Education

In January of 1992, a Baldrige Award for education was proposed. Linda James, who was the first to lead that effort in Gaithersburg, Maryland, noted that the educational initiative has developed a number of partnerships with educational associations from the American Association of School Administrators to the Association for Higher Education's Academic Quality Consortium (AQC). In addition, a group of 20 institutions were used to pilot the use of quality management principles.

The addition of the education sector to the Baldrige Award process allows educational institutions to use the criteria for self-assessment and to integrate their focus on improved results.[3]

Core Values and Concepts of the Education Pilot Criteria

The core values and concepts include:

- Learning-centered education throughout the institution
- Leadership by senior institutional officers
- Continuous improvement and organizational learning
- Faculty and staff participation in development

---

[2] Source: 1992 Handbook for the Board of Examiners. Malcolm Baldrige National Quality Award.
[3] Source: Personal Interview with Linda James. Administrator for the Baldrige Award for Education.

- Partnership development both inside and outside the institution
- Design quality and prevention
- Management by fact
- Long-range view of the future of the institution
- Public responsibility and citizenship
- Fast response both internally and externally
- Results orientation.

Education Pilot Criteria

Linkage of the Education Pilot Criteria to the Baldrige Award Criteria

The Education Pilot Criteria represent the first stage in the development of Criteria intended to focus on educational excellence. These Criteria incorporate the core values and concepts described above, and are built upon the seven-part framework used in the Baldrige Award Criteria. The rationale for the use of the same framework is that this framework defines institutional excellence and hence is adaptable to the requirements of all organizations, including educational organizations. This adaptation assumes similarity in basic requirements, but does not assume that these requirements are necessarily addressed in the same way. This initial adaptation to education, then, is largely a translation of the language and basic concepts of business excellence. A major practical benefit from using a common framework for all sectors of the economy is that it fosters cross-sector cooperation and sharing of best practices information.

Institution Assessments

The Baldrige Criteria for Education is being used as an effective assessment tool by many colleges and universities. Several accreditation associations have incorporated the Baldrige core values and concepts into their accreditation requirements.

This workbook aids an institution's assessment by keeping it simple and involving a number of faculty, staff, and students in the process. The workbook is designed to encourage participation from the institution's work force through assessment teams who ask questions and from those who answer questions against Baldrige Criteria. Total work force involvement can include up to 200 faculty, staff, and students within an institution. This assessment process helps to determine how holistically integrated the institution is in serving students and other users of its services.

CHAPTER ONE

How to Use the Workbook ___

How to Use the Baldrige Assessment Workbook

This workbook is designed to serve as an easy-to-use guide for faculty and staff cross-functional teams to assess and score their institution's quality efforts.

This workbook can be used to provide a quality check for an institution's continuous improvement efforts, to help employees understand what the Baldrige Criteria for Education are asking, and to provide a template for an institution's self-assessment and strategic planning efforts. In addition, the workbook provides guidance for employees and employee teams to score their departments or total institution in 63 areas, serves as an annual benchmark for improvement, and acts as a strategic planning guide for short-term and long-term planning. The workbook assists employees in determining their institution's readiness to apply for various quality awards. The workbook can also be used to help employees collect institutional data to write their quality award application.

How to Begin and Prepare for an Assessment

The assessment of an institution should begin with the full support and sponsorship of the chancellor, or president, and other senior institutional administrative officers. The senior leadership should appoint an assessment team administrator.

The first step in preparing for the assessment should include conducting a Baldrige assessment briefing for senior leadership. This session can be conducted by the institution's training manager or the person who has been selected as the assessment team administrator by senior institutional officers to lead the assessment process. The person(s) responsible for the briefing should review this workbook and have a thorough understanding of total quality management and the Baldrige Criteria before conducting the session.

In addition, senior leadership must be educated in the principles of total quality management (TQM) in order for them to appreciate the value of conducting an assessment. Several activities are recommended to help senior leaders develop an understanding of quality principles. These include the following:

- Reading books and articles on quality (a suggested resource list is included in Appendix C of this workbook).

- Reviewing the Malcolm Baldrige National Quality Award Criteria for Education (included throughout this workbook).

- Benchmarking other educational institutions to review best practices (see Appendixes A and B).

After senior institutional officers have been briefed, the assessment team administrator should begin the process of soliciting assessment team members. Many institutions solicit members through their faculty/staff newsletter, electronic mail, or a personal letter sent from the president inviting participation. Team member selections should be considered from a group of faculty, staff, and students who have expressed an interest in better understanding and using the Baldrige Criteria for Education as a template for improving their institution.

Once team members have been selected, a two-day assessment workshop should be conducted by faculty or staff members who have an understanding of the Baldrige Criteria. The workshop may include using a Baldrige case study for the team to practice identifying institutional strengths and opportunities for improvement in at least one or two categories (see Appendix C for case study recommendation). During the workshop, the team will discuss each category and determine "What does this mean for my institution?" The use of this workbook will help the team practice translating the Baldrige Criteria into simple language for their own institution-wide assessment.

ASSESSING THE INSTITUTION

Team Member Selection

Assessment team members should represent a cross section of faculty and staff. In addition, students should be included in the selection process. All disciplines, departments, and academic and professional levels throughout the institution should be represented on the teams. Diversity adds value and strength to each assessment team.

Team Leader Selection

In larger institutions, seven Baldrige Category sub-teams need to be developed. A subject matter expert (SME) for a particular category should be selected as the category team leader. In smaller institutions where there are a limited number of personnel who can serve on assessment teams, all categories can be assessed by one team. Following are some sample assessment team compositions.

ASSESSMENT TEAM COMPOSITION (LARGE INSTITUTION)
(20 to 40 Members)

Team 1 Leadership	Team 2 Information & Analysis	Team 3 Strategic & Operational Planning
• Chancellor or President (Team Leader) • Vice-President • Dean • Department Head • Faculty/Staff • Student	• VP - Information Systems (Team Leader) • Dean • Department Head • Faculty • Staff • Student	• VP - Finance (Team Leader) • Dean • Department Head • Faculty • Staff • Student

Team 4 Human Resource Development & Management Process	Team 5 Educational & Business Process Management	Team 6 Institutional Performance Results	Team 7 Satisfaction of Those Receiving Services
• VP - Human Resources (Team Leader) • Dean • Department Head • Faculty • Staff • Student	• VP - Academic Affairs (Team Leader) • Dean • Department Head • Faculty • Staff • Student	• VP - Finance (Team Leader) • Dean • Department Head • Faculty • Staff • Student	• VP - Student Development (Team Leader) • Dean • Department Head • Faculty • Staff • Student

ASSESSMENT TEAM COMPOSITION (SMALL INSTITUTION)
(6 to 8 members)

Team Assesses All Seven Baldrige Categories
• Provost or Vice-President (Team Leader)   • Dean   • Department Head   • Faculty (one or two)   • Staff (one or two)   • Student

Pre-assessment Meeting for Each Team

Each team will need to hold a pre-assessment planning meeting to identify individuals to be interviewed during the assessment. Dates and interview times need to be agreed upon during this session and an agenda and timetable should be prepared. After the team selects the individuals to be interviewed, a team member needs to contact all persons to be interviewed.

Coordination of Assessment Team Schedules

The assessment team administrator should coordinate all seven category team schedules with team leaders and develop an overall assessment plan and timetable. This schedule and timetable should then be submitted to the senior leadership of the institution for review and approval.

Team Interview of Selected Participants

After approval has been secured from senior leadership, each team is ready to begin its interview process with its selected participants. The entire category team will take turns interviewing the participants. This allows for more interaction and input for the assessment team. During the interview process all assessment team members will have a copy of this workbook in hand and will make notes under each of the questions. Each category team may choose to interview two to three groups of participants representing various levels throughout the institution. Interview hints and tips are provided in Appendix D.

Assessment Team Consensus and Scoring of the Category

After all category interviews have been completed, the category team leaders will hold a consensus review meeting in which all team members will review the findings regarding areas identified as strengths and opportunities for improvement. The team will reach a consensus and assign each item a percentile score and will ultimately award the category a total point score. A quick and easy institutional assessment is provided (see Appendix A) to help determine to what extent an institution has approached and deployed TQM throughout its organization. This quick assessment may be used as a preliminary analysis of one's own institution or to benchmark other institutions' TQM progress.

Entire Assessment Report Consolidated and Delivered

All seven category teams will deliver their assessment to the assessment team administrator. The assessment team administrator will meet with all category team leaders to review results.

After the assessment team administrator and all seven category team leaders have reached a consensus on the strengths, opportunities for improvement, category percentile scores and the overall assessment point score, the assessment is finalized. The completed assessment is then delivered to the chancellor or president and the other senior institutional officers. The entire assessment process can take as little as a month or as much as two months to complete.

SEVEN STEPS FOR SUCCESSFUL ASSESSMENT IMPLEMENTATION AND WORKBOOK USE

The following seven steps will further explain how this workbook will be useful in simplifying the assessment process for the institution.

STEP ONE | READ BALDRIGE CRITERIA

After the team or teams have been formed, members should read the Baldrige Award Criteria that appear at the beginning of each item throughout this workbook. Under each item summary the Baldrige Criteria for Education appear under the heading *Areas to Address.*

Leadership **41**

1.3 Public Responsibility and Citizenship (20 points) ← Item

Describe how the institution includes its responsibilities to the public in its performance improvement practices. Describe also how the institution leads and contributes as an organizational citizen in its key communities. ← Item Summary

AREAS TO ADDRESS

a. how the institution includes its public responsibilities in its performance evaluation and improvement efforts. Describe: (1) the risks and regulatory and other legal requirements addressed in planning and in setting operational requirements and targets; (2) how the institution looks ahead to anticipate public concerns associated with its operations; and (3) how the institution promotes legal and ethical conduct in its operation

b. how the institution serves as a role model in areas of public interest and concern

← Baldrige Award Criteria for Education

1.3 PERCENT SCORE

☑ Approach ☑ Deployment ☐ Results

The Baldrige Criteria notes have been eliminated but incorporated into the simplified questions throughout the workbook.

STEP TWO | REVIEW QUESTIONS

Following the *Areas to Address* pages of the workbook are questions based on the Baldrige Criteria for Education. This workbook takes all Baldrige Criteria and breaks them down into simple questions so they are more understandable and user friendly. This allows a clearer and more precise institutional assessment to be conducted.

   The questions are to be asked to different levels of faculty and staff throughout the institution. The assessment team should divide this task among its members.

Simplified questions based on Baldrige Education Criteria and rewritten for colleges and universities

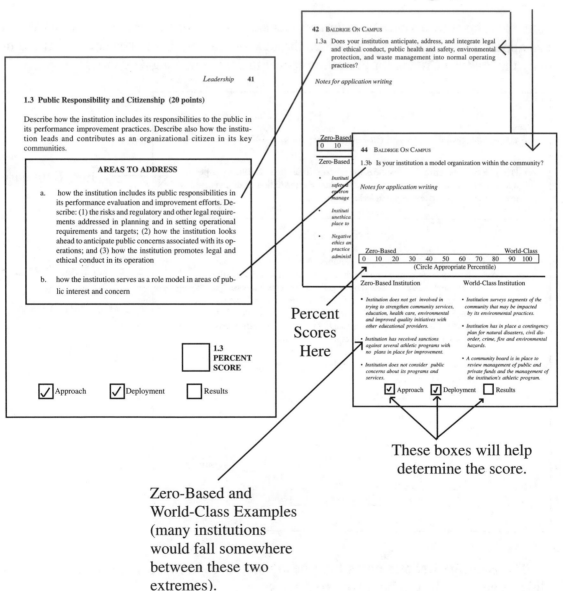

Percent Scores Here

These boxes will help determine the score.

Zero-Based and World-Class Examples (many institutions would fall somewhere between these two extremes).

STEP THREE	REVIEW ZERO-BASED & WORLD-CLASS EXAMPLES

Before recording answers to the questions, review the examples of *zero-based* institutions and *world-class* institutions that appear on the bottom third of the page.

Below the examples at the bottom of the page appear three boxes labelled *Approach, Deployment,* and *Results.* These boxes will aid in assessing the kinds of information and/or data the question requires. (Refer to chapter two—Assessment Scoring System.)

STEP FOUR	MAKE NOTES FOR APPLICATION WRITING

In the middle of the page under each question is an *application writing* section for recording answers to the questions given by faculty and staff members as they are being interviewed by the assessment team. This data should be used for writing the institution's quality award application.

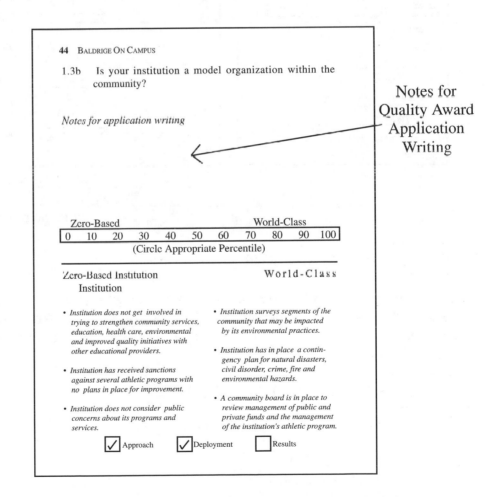

44 BALDRIGE ON CAMPUS

1.3b   Is your institution a model organization within the community?

Notes for application writing

Notes for
Quality Award
Application
Writing

Zero-Based   World-Class

| 0 | 10 | 20 | 30 | 40 | 50 | 60 | 70 | 80 | 90 | 100 |

(Circle Appropriate Percentile)

Zero-Based Institution   World-Class
   Institution

- *Institution does not get involved in trying to strengthen community services, education, health care, environmental and improved quality initiatives with other educational providers.*

- *Institution has received sanctions against several athletic programs with no plans in place for improvement.*

- *Institution does not consider public concerns about its programs and services.*

- *Institution surveys segments of the community that may be impacted by its environmental practices.*

- *Institution has in place a contingency plan for natural disasters, civil disorder, crime, fire and environmental hazards.*

- *A community board is in place to review management of public and private funds and the management of the institution's athletic program.*

☑ Approach   ☑ Deployment   ☐ Results

STEP FIVE   LIST COMMENTS FOR STRENGTHS AND IMPROVEMENT

On the opposing page the question is restated. After the interviews are completed, review the notes for application writing. The team will then list strengths and opportunities for improvement. All comments should be written in short, complete sentence form.

Comments should be written
in complete sentences.

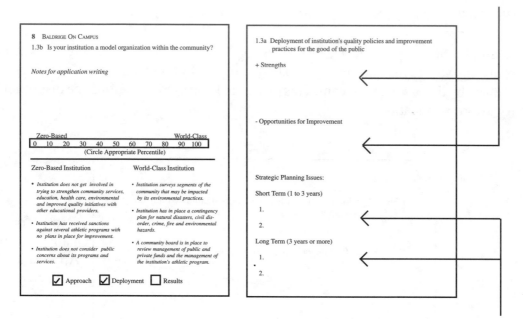

List short-term and long-term
strategic planning issues.

STEP SIX   LIST STRATEGIC PLANNING ISSUES

After reviewing the notes for application writing, strengths, and opportunities for improvement, the assessment team should select and list any short-term and long-term strategic planning issues. This data can be used later when developing a strategic plan for the institution.

STEP SEVEN   SCORE ASSESSMENT ITEMS

The assessment is broken down into seven Baldrige Categories:

1.0.   Leadership
2.0.   Information and Analysis
3.0.   Strategic and Operational Planning

4.0. Human Resource Development and Management
5.0. Educational and Business Process Management
6.0. Institution's Performance Results
7.0. Satisfaction of Those Receiving Services

These seven categories are divided into 28 assessment items (i.e., 1.1, 1.2, 1.3, 2.1, 2.2 . . .) and the 28 assessment items are broken down into 63 areas (i.e., 1.1a, 1.1b, . . .). The percent score is reflective of the strengths and opportunities for improvement of the areas within each assessment item. Thus, throughout the assessment all 28 items will obtain a percent score. All assessment item percent scores will be transferred to the Summary of Assessment Items score sheet located at the end of chapter nine. A graph illustrating the hierarchy of institutional needs, based on the Baldrige Criteria for Higher Education, helps visually present the percent scores of each assessment category.

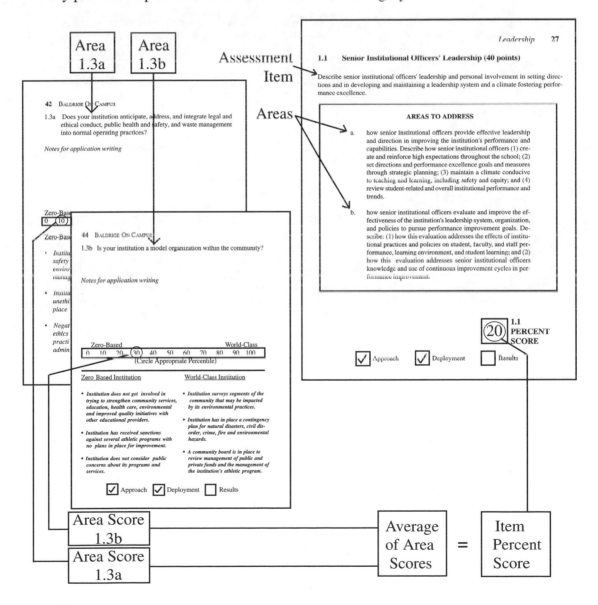

The assessment scores will ultimately be reviewed, prioritized, and transformed into actionable strategies for improvement. The transformation process is explained in detail in chapter ten of the workbook.

CHAPTER TWO

Assessment Scoring System ___

The Baldrige scoring system is based on three evaluation dimensions: (1) Approach, (2) Deployment, and (3) Results. All three dimensions should be considered before assigning a percentage score. In addition, each of the categories assessed will have *Scoring Profiles* to help facilitate the scoring process.[4]

Approach

Approach refers to the methods the institution uses to achieve purposes addressed in the Assessment Categories. The scoring criteria used to evaluate approaches include one or more of the following, as appropriate:

- The appropriateness of the methods, tools, and techniques to the requirements

- The effectiveness of the use of methods, tools, and techniques

- The degree to which the approach is systematic, integrated, and consistently applied

- The degree to which the approach embodies effective evaluation/improvement cycles

- The degree to which the approach is based upon quantitative information that is objective and reliable

- The degree to which the approach is prevention-based

- The indicators of unique and innovative approaches, including significant and effective new adaptations of tools and techniques used in other applications or types of organizations.

---

[4] Source: 1993 Malcolm Baldrige National Quality Award Examiners' Course Training Material. Malcolm Baldrige National Quality Award.

Deployment

Deployment refers to the extent to which the approaches are applied to all relevant areas and activities addressed and implied in the Assessment Categories. The scoring criteria used to evaluate deployment include one or more of the following, as appropriate:

- The appropriateness and effective application by all work units to all processes and activities

- The appropriate and effective application to all program and service features

- The appropriate and effective application to all transactions and interactions with faculty, staff, students, stakeholders, suppliers, and the public.

Results

Results refers to outcomes and effects in achieving the purposes addressed and implied in the Assessment Categories. The scoring criteria used to evaluate results include one or more of the following:

- The quality and performance levels demonstrated and their importance

- The rate of quality and performance improvement

- The breadth of quality and performance improvement

- The demonstration of sustained improvement

- The comparison with competitive institutions and other leading educational providers

- The institution's ability to show the improvements derive from its quality practices and actions.

The percent scores range from a low of 0% for a *zero-based* institution to a high of 100% for a *world-class* institution. An institution can be 0% in some areas and 100% (world-class) in others. The anchor point is 50% which is middle range. Many institutions fall below the 50% anchor point. The 50% anchor point is considered to be good, but certainly below what an institution that is striving to be the "best-in-class" among leading institutions would score.

Zero-Based					Anchor Point					World-Class
0%					50%					100%
0	10	20	30	40	(50)	60	70	80	90	100

Institutions that score 0% have an anecdotal approach, lack deployment, and have no meaningful results. Institutions that score 100% reflect a refined, very mature approach that is deployed and well adapted in all relevant areas.

Approach and Deployment

Approach and deployment are considered together. This is because without deployment, an approach would merely represent an idea or a plan. The Baldrige Criteria are based heavily upon successful quality strategies that advocate approaches that are implemented and deployed.

SCORING GUIDELINES

SCORE	APPROACH	DEPLOYMENT	RESULTS
0%	• *anecdotal, no system evident*	• *anecdotal*	• *anecdotal*
10-30%	• *beginnings of systematic prevention basis*	• *some to many major areas of institution*	• *some positive trends in the areas deployed*
40-60% (50% Anchor Point)	• *sound, systematic prevention basis that includes evaluation/ improvement cycles* • *some evidence of integration*	• *most major areas of institution* • *some support areas*	• *positive trends in most major areas* • *some evidence that results are caused by approach*
70-90%	• *sound, systematic prevention basis with evidence of refinement through evaluation/ improvement cycles* • *good integration*	• *major areas of institution* • *from some to many support areas*	• *good to excellent in major areas* • *positive trends- from some to many support areas* • *evidence that results are caused by approach*
100%	• *sound, systematic prevention basis refined through evaluation/ improvement cycles* • *excellent integration*	• *major areas and support areas* • *all operations*	• *excellent (world-class) results in major areas* • *good to excellent in support areas* • *sustained results* • *results clearly caused approach*

· INSTITUTIONAL SCORING PROFILES
(Each of the seven Baldrige Categories
are profiled into five percentile ranges.)

Scoring of the 28 Baldrige items can be difficult for an assessment team to complete. Scoring profiles are provided in this workbook to aid the team's scoring process. The teams should first consider the three dimensions (Approach, Deployment, and Results) and review the scoring guidelines on the preceding page before using the scoring profiles section. The scoring profiles will aid the team in further profiling the percentile range in which the scores should fall.[5]

   Each team should avoid merely using the scoring profiles to score without first considering approach, deployment, and results. The scores tend to be positively skewed when solely using scoring profiles without consideration of the three dimensions of scoring.

1.0 Leadership (90 points)

100 - 80%

- Senior institutional officers are visibly involved in total quality management.
- Senior institutional officers are involved and encourage teams to be formed throughout the institution and to focus on continuous improvement.
- Senior institutional officers communicate the institution's quality policies and vision with faculty and staff.
- Senior institutional officers advocate participative management throughout the institution.
- Senior institutional officers reflect commitment to public health, safety, environmental protection, institutional values, and continuous improvement efforts.

80 - 60%

- Most senior institutional officers are visibly involved in promoting quality throughout the institution.
- Senior institutional officers meet with faculty and staff groups/teams and students on quality issues.
- Commitment to public responsibility and institutional citizenship is deployed throughout the institution by senior institutional officers.
- Administrative behavior at all levels of the institution reflect quality as a major priority for the institution.
- Senior institutional officers communicate the institution's quality values, vision, and mission to faculty, staff, students, stakeholders, and suppliers.

---

[5]   Source: 1993 Board of Examiners Booklet for the President's Quality Award Program, Federal Quality Institute.

60 - 40%

- Senior institutional officers share quality values with faculty, staff, and students.
- Administrator's performance is evaluated against measurable quality strategies.
- Senior institutional officers are committed to public responsibility and institutional citizenship.
- Participative management is practiced in many parts of the institution.
- Senior institutional officers support short- and long-term strategic quality improvement.

40 - 20%

- A few senior institutional officers and other administrators support and are involved in the institution's quality improvement efforts.
- Administrators and department heads are encouraged to become involved in the institution's quality improvement efforts.
- Communication within the institution is usually vertical (top down); no cooperation across departments is encouraged.
- Institution's quality policies reflect commitment to public responsibility and institutional citizenship.
- Continuous improvement practiced in some parts of the institution.

20 - 0%

- Senior institutional officers are beginning to support the quality process.
- Quality practices are not understood in some parts of the institution.
- Senior institutional officers have not fully developed their quality vision, nor is there a quality plan in place.
- Senior institutional officers do not get involved with faculty, staff, and students in sharing the institution's quality vision.
- Public responsibility and corporate citizenship is of no concern to senior institutional officer.

2.0 Information and Analysis (75 points)

100 - 80%

- Quality-related data are available for critical processes used to produce programs/ services.
- Processes and technology that ensure timely, accurate, valid, and useful data collection for process owners are used throughout the institution.
- Data are analyzed institution-wide by faculty and staff teams that translate it into actionable information to ensure continuous quality improvement.

- Institutional comparisons and benchmarking information and data are used to help drive continuous improvement.
- Quality-related data are integrated and distributed to process owners throughout the institution.

80 - 60%

- Faculty and staff have rapid access to data in most parts of the institution.
- Processes and technologies are used across most of the institution to ensure that data are complete, timely, accurate, valid, and useful.
- Comparative data are collected, analyzed, and translated into actionable information to support decision making and planning.
- Most critical processes have data on quality, timeliness, and productivity.
- Measures exist that relate to the institution's strategic objectives for most programs/services.

60 - 40%

- Benchmark and comparative data are collected on some programs, services, and processes.
- Processes and technologies are used across many parts of the institution that ensure data are complete, timely, accurate, valid, and useful.
- Faculty and staff have access to data in many parts of the organization.
- Many critical processes have data on quality, timeliness, and productivity.
- Measures exist that relate to the institution's strategic objectives for many programs/services.

40 - 20%

- Data exist for some critical programs/services and processes.
- Data are limited on many major processes.
- Data are collected on some students, stakeholders, and suppliers.
- Centralized group analyzes data, faculty, and staff teams not used for data analysis.
- Limited process controls are in place to ensure that data analysis is used to drive improvement within the institution.

20 - 0%

- Data received for comparison appear anecdotal.
- Data received are used primarily for reporting purposes, not for improvement.
- Data are limited for a select few critical processes.
- None or very little student and stakeholder or supplier data are used for improvement.
- Data analysis is in beginning stages of use for the institution's improvement efforts.

3.0 Strategic and Operational Planning (75 points)

100 - 80%

- Strategic planning is used to develop quality improvement goals throughout the institution.
- All faculty, staff, and students give input to strategic planning process.
- Faculty, staff, students, customers, and suppliers are fully involved in planning process.
- All administrative levels' activity is involved in planning process.
- Strategic planning process includes short-term and long-term plans based on key quality data, student and stakeholder data, faculty/staff survey data, supplier and benchmark data that are deployed throughout the institution.

80 - 60%

- Strategic plans for quality improvement relating to mission, vision, and values are established across the institution.
- Institution uses a broad planning process that involves faculty, staff, students, stakeholders, and suppliers.
- Strategic planning process includes short-term and long-term plans based on key quality data, student and stakeholder data, faculty/staff survey data, supplier and benchmark data that are deployed throughout the institution.
- Senior institutional officers provide input and approve strategic plan.
- Operational plans developed throughout the institution are linked to the master strategic plan; administrators are held accountable for meeting strategic goals.

60 - 40%

- Operational plans are developed at divisional levels that link with institution's strategic plan.
- Administrators at all levels are held accountable for deploying strategic plan.
- Organization involves faculty, staff, students, supplier, and stakeholders in planning process.
- Strategic planning process includes short-term and long-term plans based on some quality data, student and stakeholder data, faculty/staff survey data, supplier and benchmark data that are deployed throughout most parts of the institution.
- Strategic planning process is deployed across the institution and approved by senior institutional officers.

40 - 20%

- Strategic goals are established for key functional areas of the institution.
- A strategic planning process is in place within the institution.

- Senior institutional officers approve strategic plan.
- Some students, stakeholders, and suppliers are involved in strategic planning process.
- Administrators provide student and stakeholder data for the strategic planning process.

20 - 0%

- None-to-very-few students, stakeholders, or suppliers are involved in the institution's strategic planning process.
- Personnel at lower levels of institution are not involved in planning process.
- Strategic planning is not mentioned nor understood throughout the institution.
- The institution's plan is developed by senior institutional officers with no input from faculty, staff, students, suppliers, or stakeholders.
- The strategic plan has no student and stakeholder involvement, or student and stakeholder focus.

4.0 Human Resource Development and Management (150 points)

100 - 80%

- Institution has fully implemented and deployed faculty and staff, growth and development plans, education, training, and empowerment plans with measurement results.
- Institution has documented favorable trends regarding percent of faculty and staff recognized for individual and team contributions. Recognition is tied to the institution's quality goals and strategic plan.
- Positive trends shown within past few years with team involvement regarding improved work processes throughout the institution.
- Faculty/staff innovations, cross-functional teams, and natural work groups encouraged throughout the institution.
- Institution is highly sensitive to faculty and staff well-being and satisfaction.

80 - 60%

- Senior institutional officers and most administrators support faculty and staff involvement, contributions, and teamwork.
- Teams and faculty and staff work groups feel a strong sense of empowerment and practice innovations across most parts of the institution.
- Faculty and staff have rapid access to data through their computer networks in most parts of the institution.
- Faculty and staff idea sharing is encouraged and acted upon by administrators across most parts of the organization.
- Institution maintains a work environment conducive to the well-being and growth of the work force.

40 - 20%

- Faculty and staff empowerment is not encouraged in all divisions of the institution.
- Rewards and recognition are not deployed fully among all employee levels; more focused on individual, as opposed to team, contributions.
- Not all faculty and staff development and training initiatives are connected with the institution's quality plans and objectives.
- Administrators in some parts of the institution support faculty and staff involvement and empowerment.
- Institution not consistently supportive of a work environment conducive to the well-being and growth of the work force.

20 - 0%

- Institution does not offer training on a consistent basis.
- Few employees are empowered or work in teams within the institution.
- Faculty and staff rewards and recognition do not appear to be focused on the institution's quality plan and goals for continuous improvement.
- Faculty and staff development is not a priority initiative within the institution.
- Some administrators support faculty and staff involvement and participative management.

5.0 Educational and Business Process Management (150 points)

100 - 80%

- Work processes are documented and controlled across the institution.
- Systematic approaches are used throughout the institution to ensure shortened cycle-time and consistent programs and services.
- Critical supplier partnerships are formed or supplier certification programs are in place to ensure consistency of all processes throughout the institution.
- Periodic assessments of critical processes are conducted.
- Analytic problem solving tools are used throughout the institution to identify and solve process problems.

80 - 60%

- Processes are documented and controlled across most parts of the institution.
- Systematic approaches are used throughout most parts of the institution to ensure shortened cycle-time and consistent programs and services.
- Supplier quality is a main consideration when selecting critical suppliers.
- Comprehensive assessments are conducted consistently throughout the institution to ensure that all processes are meeting student and stakeholder requirements.
- Analytic problem solving tools are used in most parts of the institution to identify and solve process problems.

60 - 40%

- Institution uses stakeholder data (i.e., survey data, focus groups) to design processes for new/improved programs and services in many parts of the institution.
- Critical suppliers are required to meet documented standards in many parts of the institution.
- Problem-solving tools are used in many parts of the institution.
- Process assessments are conducted in many parts of the institution.
- Standardized preventative measures to ensure quality programs/services are used in many parts of the institution.

40 - 20%

- In most parts of the institution appraisal is emphasized as opposed to prevention.
- Cost is the primary consideration in choosing suppliers.
- Quality assessments of core processes are conducted only when processes are out of control on a consistent basis.
- Problem-solving tools are used in some parts of the institution.
- Some student and customer input is sought to improve processes.

20 - 0%

- Systematic approaches to ensure reduced cycle time and improved processes are delegated to a single department.
- No student and stakeholder or supplier input is sought to improve the institution's core processes.
- Suppliers are not considered partners in quality within the institution.
- Very few or no problem-solving tools are used to identify and solve process problems.
- Institution is in appraisal mode versus prevention mode.

6.0 Institution's Performance Results (230 points)

100 - 80%

- Student and stakeholder satisfaction surveys show positive trends over the past two to three years.
- Supplier data show improvement over the past two to three years.
- Positive results are shown in reduced cycle-time and productivity improvement across the institution in programs and services over the past two to three years.
- Improvement plans are in place in areas of the institution that show negative trends.
- Administrative and support services show improved results and positive trends over the past two to three years.

80 - 60%

- Most operational performance levels demonstrate positive results over the past two to three years.
- Results indicate some institutional suppliers have improved over the past two to three years.
- Results reflect improvement in cycle-time and operational performance.
- Benchmark results reveal that the institution is leading other educational providers in several core processes.
- Key measures of administrative and support services reflecting principal quality, productivity, cycle-time, and cost results have improved over the past two to three years in most parts of the institution.

60 - 40%

- Student and customer satisfaction surveys reflect positive results over the past two to three years.
- Critical institutional suppliers are meeting quality standards with a few showing positive results over the past two years.
- Comparisons and benchmarks are conducted within key areas of the institution and benchmark results are documented.
- Key measures of operational, program, and service results are captured in critical areas of the institution. Positive results are reflected over the past two to three years.
- Competitive comparisons are made within the institution that reflect positive one-to-two-year results.

40 - 20%

- Program service measures reflect improved trends.
- Student and stakeholder satisfaction surveys reflect improvement.
- Some suppliers are meeting the institution's documented quality standards.
- Improved results in cycle-time and improved programs/services documented in some parts of the institution.
- Measurement is not fully deployed across the institution.

20 - 0%

- Anecdotal evidence of improvement is shown.
- Student and stakeholder satisfaction is not measured.
- Improvements are measured in few, if any, parts of the institution.
- Supplier improvement is not measured or considered.
- No benchmarking or comparisons are conducted.

7.0 Satisfaction of Those Receiving Services (230 points)

100 - 80%

- Student and stakeholder surveys, focus groups, and exit interviews are used to determine satisfaction, repurchase intentions, and satisfaction relative to other educational providers.
- Administration is actively focused on ensuring an internal/external, student/stakeholder focus throughout the institution.
- Student and stakeholder-contact training is required throughout the institution for faculty and staff who interface with students and stakeholders.
- Institution promotes trust and confidence in its program/services.
- Institution is continuously determining short-term and long-term student and stakeholder requirements and expectations.

80 - 60%

- Effective feedback systems are in place to obtain critical student and stakeholder data for continuous improvement.
- Administration promotes and deploys an internal/external student and stakeholder focus throughout the institution.
- Senior institutional officers are approachable for students and stakeholders.
- Specific student and stakeholder-contact training is in place.
- Logistical support is in place for student and stakeholder-contact employees.

60 - 40%

- Student and stakeholder survey data are deployed throughout the institution to drive continuous improvement in programs/services.
- Student and stakeholder-contact employees are trained.
- Internal/external stakeholder focus is promoted throughout the institution.
- Student and stakeholder focus and satisfaction issues tie in with the institution's short-term and long-term strategic plans.
- Effective systems are in place in many programs/services linking internal/external student and stakeholder feedback to employee teams.

40 - 20%

- Most internal/external stakeholders/customers are identified; needs/expectations are not determined through a systematic process.
- Some students and stakeholder groups are segmented.
- Student and stakeholder service standards are revised periodically for some programs/services.

- Senior institutional officers are rarely accessible to students and stakeholders.
- Future student and stakeholder expectations are not determined or considered in the institution's short-term and long-term planning process.

20 - 0%

- Few, if any, student and stakeholder service standards have been established by the institution.
- Student and stakeholder service focus is on problem solving.
- Student and stakeholder feedback is not always considered when developing or improving programs/services.
- Student and stakeholder complaints are major method for obtaining student and stakeholder feedback.
- Institution does not promote trust and confidence in its programs/services.

The preceding scoring profiles, in addition to being used to help determine each item score, can also be helpful to the team when reviewing each category. These scoring profiles can serve as a benchmark for the team to review holistically an entire category and compare the assessment strengths and opportunities for improvement against the profiled category percentile ranges.

This chapter should be reviewed by the assessment team before attempting to score and reach a consensus on each item. The team must remember to review approach, deployment, and results of each item and the scoring guidelines before incorporating the scoring profiles into the determination of the ultimate score.

CHAPTER THREE

Category 1.0
Leadership ⎯⎯⎯⎯⎯⎯⎯

1.0   Leadership (90 points)[6]

The Leadership Category examines institutional administrators' personal leadership and involvement in creating and sustaining a student focus, clear goals, high expectations, and a leadership system that promotes performance excellence. Also examined is how these objectives and expectations are integrated into the institution's management system.

---

[6]   Source: Leadership Category 1.0 has been rewritten and revised for institutions of higher education and simplified based on the 1995 Malcolm Baldrige National Quality Award Education Pilot Criteria.

1.1 Senior Institutional Officers' Leadership (40 points)

Describe senior institutional officers' leadership and personal involvement in setting directions and in developing and maintaining a leadership system and a climate fostering performance excellence.

AREAS TO ADDRESS

a. how senior institutional officers provide effective leadership and direction in improving the institution's performance and capabilities. Describe how senior institutional officers: (1) create and reinforce high expectations throughout the school; (2) set directions and performance excellence goals and measures through strategic planning; (3) maintain a climate conducive to teaching and learning, including safety and equity; and (4) review student-related and overall institutional performance and trends.

b. how senior institutional officers evaluate and improve the effectiveness of the institution's leadership system, organization, and policies to pursue performance improvement goals. Describe: (1) how this evaluation addresses the effects of institutional practices and policies on student, faculty, and staff performance, learning environment, and student learning; and (2) how this evaluation addresses senior institutional officers knowledge and use of continuous improvement cycles in performance improvement.

1.1 PERCENT SCORE

 Approach    Deployment   Results

1.1a   To what extent are senior institutional officers involved in fostering your institution's quality excellence (e.g., creating and promoting values, strategic planning and goal setting, promoting and maintaining a learning environment, reviewing performance trends and relating these trends to continuous improvement)?

Notes for application writing:

Zero-Based   World-Class

0	10	20	30	40	50	60	70	80	90	100

(Circle Appropriate Percentile)

Zero-Based Institution

- *Not all senior institutional officers are personally involved in promoting quality values throughout the institution.*

- *Senior institutional officers are not involved in recognizing faculty and staff members who promote a learning environment.*

- *Senior institutional officers do not promote safety and equity throughout the institution.*

World-Class Institution

- *Senior institutional officers are personally and visibly involved in deploying a customer-focused environment for students, faculty, and staff throughout the institution.*

- *Institution has a published values statement that is promoted by all senior institutional officers.*

- *Senior institutional officers communicated the institution's student and other customer service orientation and quality values through articles in the campus newsletter and internal/external speeches.*

☑ Approach   ☑ Deployment   ☐ Results

1.1a   Senior institutional officers' personal involvement in setting directions and fostering performance excellence.

+ Strengths

1.

2.

3.

- Opportunities for Improvement

1.

2.

3.

Strategic Planning Issues:

   Short Term (1 to 2 years)

   1.

   2.

   Long Term (2 years or more)

   1.

   2.

1.1b   How do senior institutional officers evaluate and improve the institution's leadership system, organization, and policies?

Notes for application writing:

Zero-Based   World-Class

0	10	20	30	40	50	60	70	80	90	100

(Circle Appropriate Percentile)

Zero-Based Institution

- *The institution's leadership effectiveness is not assessed by peers, colleagues, advisory bodies, or governing boards.*

- *Senior institutional officers have not designed or utilized an assessment process to evaluate the institution's leadership system, organization, and policies.*

- *No process is in place that evaluates how senior institutional officers focus on continuous improvement throughout the institution to foster performance excellence.*

World-Class Institution

- *Direct report staff rates senior institutional officers annually with a leadership questionnaire.*

- *Annual faculty and staff satisfaction survey is conducted by a third party to evaluate leadership effectiveness and personal involvement of senior institutional officers.*

- *Senior institutional officers review annually, with input from students, faculty, and staff, the institution's organizational structure and policies to ensure performance excellence and the promotion of a continuous learning environment throughout the institution.*

☑ Approach   ☑ Deployment   ☐ Results

1.1b   Senior institutional officers evaluate and improve the institution's leadership system, organization, and policies.

+ Strengths

1.

2.

3.

- Opportunities for Improvement

1.

2.

3.

Strategic Planning Issues:

Short Term (1 to 2 years)

1.

2.

Long Term (2 years or more)

1.

2.

1.2 NOTES

1.2 Leadership System and Organization (30 points)

Describe how the institution's student focus and performance expectations are integrated into the institution's leadership system, organization, and policies.

AREAS TO ADDRESS

a. how the institution's leadership system, management, organization, and policies focus on student and overall institutional performance improvement objectives. Describe: (1) how these objectives are incorporated into institutional practices; and (2) how the institution maintains focus and cooperation among units to pursue these objectives.

b. how the institution effectively communicates and regularly reinforces its directions and expectations throughout the institutional community. Describe policies and practices that reflect the expectations and directions.

c. how overall institution and individual unit performance are reviewed and how the reviews are used to improve performance. Describe: (1) the types, frequency, and content of reviews and who conducts them; (2) how the results of reviews are used to strengthen awareness and use of learning-oriented assessment in all education programs.

**1.2
PERCENT
SCORE**

 Approach    Deployment   ☐ Results

1.2a   Does your institution's leadership, management, and organizational structure and policies support student development, achievement, and improved performance?

Notes for application writing:

Zero-Based   World-Class

0	10	20	30	40	50	60	70	80	90	100

(Circle Appropriate Percentile)

Zero-Based Institution

- *Institution's organizational structure and policies do not support student growth and development.*

- *A few departments have restructured to focus on student growth and development.*

- *Few policies exist that promote and focus on student development, achievement, and performance improvement.*

World-Class Institution

- *Institution has realigned all management and staff positions to focus on improved student development and achievement.*

- *Institution promotes cooperation among all departments and divisions in shortening cycle-time for student services.*

- *Faculty and staff focus groups are formed within each division to review policies that do not promote student development, achievement, and improved performance.*

☑ Approach   ☑ Deployment   ☐ Results

1.2a   Institution's leadership, management, and organizational structure and policies promote student growth and development.

+ Strengths

1.

2.

3.

- Opportunities for Improvement

1.

2.

3.

Strategic Planning Issues:

   Short Term (1 to 2 years)

   1.

   2.

   Long Term (2 years or more)

   1.

   2.

1.2b   Do senior institutional officers communicate and regularly reinforce the institution's student focus, values, expectations, and directives throughout the institution among faculty and staff?

Notes for application writing:

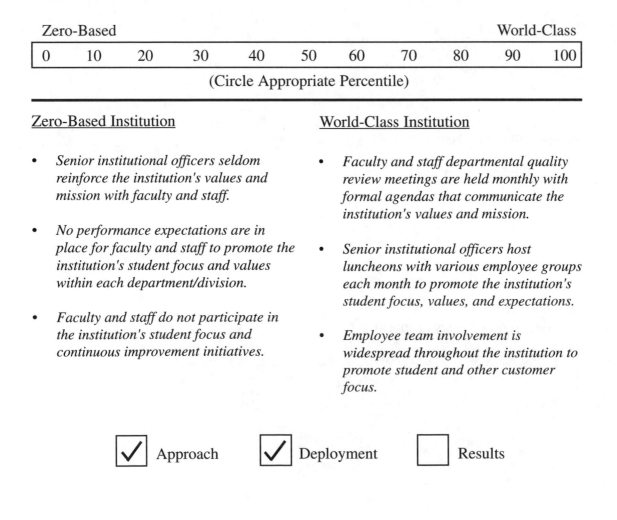

Zero-Based   World-Class

| 0 | 10 | 20 | 30 | 40 | 50 | 60 | 70 | 80 | 90 | 100 |

(Circle Appropriate Percentile)

Zero-Based Institution

- *Senior institutional officers seldom reinforce the institution's values and mission with faculty and staff.*

- *No performance expectations are in place for faculty and staff to promote the institution's student focus and values within each department/division.*

- *Faculty and staff do not participate in the institution's student focus and continuous improvement initiatives.*

World-Class Institution

- *Faculty and staff departmental quality review meetings are held monthly with formal agendas that communicate the institution's values and mission.*

- *Senior institutional officers host luncheons with various employee groups each month to promote the institution's student focus, values, and expectations.*

- *Employee team involvement is widespread throughout the institution to promote student and other customer focus.*

☑ Approach   ☑ Deployment   ☐ Results

1.2b   Senior institutional officers' reinforcement and communication of student focus and institutional values among faculty and staff.

+ Strengths

1.

2.

3.

- Opportunities for Improvement

1.

2.

3.

Strategic Planning Issues:

Short Term (1 to 2 years)

1.

2.

Long Term (2 years or more)

1.

2.

1.2c   Does your institution review the awareness and integration of student/customer quality values at all levels/departments/divisions? Are the results of these evaluations used to implement changes in your institution's leadership approach to achieve better results?

Notes for application writing:

Zero-Based   World-Class

| 0 | 10 | 20 | 30 | 40 | 50 | 60 | 70 | 80 | 90 | 100 |

(Circle Appropriate Percentile)

Zero-Based Institution	World-Class Institution
• *Senior institutional officers' involvement in quality initiatives throughout the institution does not exist.*	• *The institution conducts an overall annual assessment and reviews results with all faculty and staff.*
• *Faculty and staff do not participate in the institutional review.*	• *Faculty and staff involvement in reviewing unit performance is widespread throughout the institution.*
• *Institution does not review work unit quality and operational performance.*	• *Review teams are composed of cross-functional faculty and staff who review daily nonconformance.*

 ☑ Approach   ☑ Deployment   ☐ Results

1.2c   Institution's review of plans and goals organization-wide to improve performance.

+ Strengths

1.

2.

3.

- Opportunities for Improvement

1.

2.

3.

Strategic Planning Issues:

    Short Term (1 to 2 years)

      1.

      2.

    Long Term (2 years or more)

      1.

      2.

1.3 NOTES

1.3 Public Responsibility and Citizenship (20 points)

Describe how the institution includes its responsibilities to the public in its performance improvement practices. Describe also how the institution leads and contributes as an organizational citizen in its key communities.

AREAS TO ADDRESS

a. how the institution includes its public responsibilities in its performance evaluation and improvement efforts. Describe: (1) the risks and regulatory and other legal requirements addressed in planning and in setting operational requirements and targets; (2) how the institution looks ahead to anticipate public concerns associated with its operations; and (3) how the institution promotes legal and ethical conduct in its operation.

b. how the institution serves as a role model in areas of public interest and concern.

1.3 PERCENT SCORE

 Approach  Deployment ☐ Results

1.3a   Does your institution anticipate, address, and integrate legal and ethical conduct, public health and safety, environmental protection, and waste management into normal operating practices?

Notes for application writing:

Zero-Based   World-Class

0	10	20	30	40	50	60	70	80	90	100

(Circle Appropriate Percentile)

Zero-Based Institution

- *Institution does not promote employee safety and does not address environmental protection and waste management in its daily practices.*

- *Institution has been cited for unsafe and unethical conduct and has no plan in place to address improvement.*

- *Negative publicity about institutional ethics and environmental and safety practices are of no concern to the administration.*

World-Class Institution

- *Institution surveys segments of the community that may be impacted by its programs, services, and operations.*

- *Institution has established community focus groups that meet annually to address any concerns about the institution's operating practices.*

- *Faculty and staff are encouraged to promote quality initiatives in local, state, and national agencies and organizations.*

 Approach   ✓ Deployment   ☐ Results

1.3a   Deployment of institution's quality policies and improvement practices for the good of the public.

+ Strengths

1.

2.

3.

- Opportunities for Improvement

1.

2.

3.

Strategic Planning Issues:

    Short Term (1 to 2 years)

        1.

        2.

    Long Term (2 years or more)

        1.

        2.

1.3b   Is your institution a model organization within the community?

Notes for application writing:

Zero-Based   World-Class

| 0 | 10 | 20 | 30 | 40 | 50 | 60 | 70 | 80 | 90 | 100 |

(Circle Appropriate Percentile)

Zero-Based Institution

- *Institution does not get involved in trying to strengthen community services, education, health care, environmental and improved quality initiatives with other educational providers.*

- *Institution has received sanctions against several athletic programs with no plans in place for improvement.*

- *Institution does not consider public concerns about its programs and services.*

World-Class Institution

- *Institution surveys segments of the community that may be impacted by its environmental practices.*

- *Institution has in place a contingency plan for natural disasters, civil disorder, crime, fire, and environmental hazards.*

- *A community board is in place to review management of public and private funds and the management of the institution's athletic program.*

 Approach   ✓ Deployment   ☐ Results

1.3b   Institution as a model organization within the community.

+ Strengths

1.

2.

3.

- Opportunities for Improvement

1.

2.

3.

Strategic Planning Issues:

   Short Term (1 to 2 years)

   1.

   2.

   Long Term (2 years or more)

   1.

   2.

CHAPTER FOUR

Category 2.0
Information and Analysis——

2.0 Information and Analysis (75 points)[7]

The Information and Analysis Category examines the management and effectiveness of use of data and information to support overall mission-related performance excellence.

---

[7] Source: Information and Analysis Category 2.0 Criteria has been rewritten and revised for institutions of higher education and simplified based on the 1995 Malcolm Baldrige National Quality Award Education Pilot Criteria.

2.1 Management of Information and Data (25 points)

Describe the institution's selection and management of information and data used for planning, management, and evaluation of overall institutional performance improvement.

AREAS TO ADDRESS

a. how information and data needed to drive improvement of education and business operational performance are elected and managed. Describe: (1) the rationale for the main types of information and data used to drive and to track educational progress; (2) the rationale for the main types of information and data used to drive and to track business operational performance; and (3) how needs such as reliability, rapid access, rapid update, and privacy are addressed.

b. how the institution evaluates and improves the selection, analysis, and integration of information and data, aligning them with the institution's priorities. Describe how the evaluation considers: (1) scope of information and data; (2) analysis and use of information and data to support overall performance improvement; and (3) feedback from users of information and data.

2.1
PERCENT
SCORE

 Approach    Deployment   ☐ Results

2.1a Does your institution select and manage reliable data that all faculty and staff can understand? Data by categories might include:
1. Student and other customer data
2. Program and service performance data
3. Survey data

Notes for application writing:

Zero-Based   World-Class

0	10	20	30	40	50	60	70	80	90	100

(Circle Appropriate Percentile)

Zero-Based Institution

- *Data that are measured are not presented in a "user-friendly" format for faculty and staff to understand.*

- *Data are disseminated to faculty and staff on an inconsistent basis.*

- *No strategic plan in place to prioritize and coordinate data collection throughout the institution.*

World-Class Institution

- *Data gathering supports institution's quality initiatives.*

- *All faculty and staff have rapid access to reliable, consistent data through their personal computers located in each division and department.*

- *Data and information collection are aligned with institution's cycle-time reduction plans and needs.*

 ✓ Approach ✓ Deployment ☐ Results

2.1a   Institution's selection and management of data.

+ Strengths

1.

2.

3.

- Opportunities for Improvement

1.

2.

3.

Strategic Planning Issues:

    Short Term (1 to 2 years)

      1.

      2.

    Long Term (2 years or more)

      1.

      2.

2.1b   How does your institution select, analyze, and integrate data to support improved operational and academic performance?

Notes for application writing:

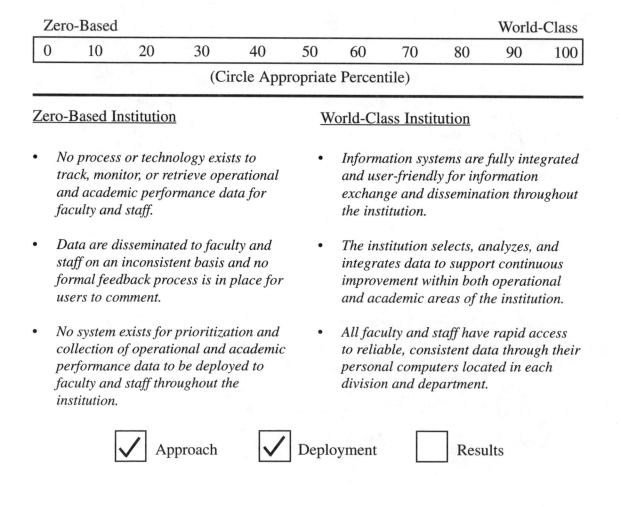

Zero-Based   World-Class

0	10	20	30	40	50	60	70	80	90	100

(Circle Appropriate Percentile)

Zero-Based Institution

- *No process or technology exists to track, monitor, or retrieve operational and academic performance data for faculty and staff.*

- *Data are disseminated to faculty and staff on an inconsistent basis and no formal feedback process is in place for users to comment.*

- *No system exists for prioritization and collection of operational and academic performance data to be deployed to faculty and staff throughout the institution.*

World-Class Institution

- *Information systems are fully integrated and user-friendly for information exchange and dissemination throughout the institution.*

- *The institution selects, analyzes, and integrates data to support continuous improvement within both operational and academic areas of the institution.*

- *All faculty and staff have rapid access to reliable, consistent data through their personal computers located in each division and department.*

☑ Approach   ☑ Deployment   ☐ Results

2.1b　Institution's use of data supports improved operational and academic performance.

+ Strengths

1.

2.

3.

- Opportunities for Improvement

1.

2.

3.

Strategic Planning Issues:

　Short Term (1 to 2 years)

　　1.

　　2.

　Long Term (2 years or more)

　　1.

　　2.

2.2 NOTES

2.2 Comparisons and Benchmarking (15 points)

Describe the institution's processes for selecting and using comparative information and data to support overall performance improvement.

AREAS TO ADDRESS

a. how comparisons and benchmarking information and data are selected and used to help drive improvement of overall school performance. Describe: (1) how needs and priorities are determined; (2) criteria for seeking appropriate information and data—from within and outside the academic community; (3) how the benchmarking information and data are used within the school to improve understanding of processes and process performance; and (4) how the information and data are used to set improvement targets and/or encourage breakthrough approaches.

b. how the institution evaluates and improves its overall process for selecting and using comparisons and benchmarking information and data to improve planning and overall institutional performance.

2.2
PERCENT
SCORE

 Approach   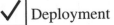 Deployment   ☐ Results

2.2a   Does your institution compare data against and benchmark other educational providers and non-academic organizations? How does your institution select and use comparison and benchmark data for overall improvement?

Notes for application writing:

Zero-Based   World-Class

| 0 | 10 | 20 | 30 | 40 | 50 | 60 | 70 | 80 | 90 | 100 |

(Circle Appropriate Percentile)

Zero-Based Institution

- *No comparisons or benchmarks are conducted.*

- *Comparison and benchmark data are selected and used only as a public relations tool for the institution to showcase various programs.*

- *Comparison and benchmark data are not selected and used for improvement in academic programs and overall operations.*

World-Class Institution

- *Comparisons and benchmarks are conducted throughout the institution to improve selected programs and student support services.*

- *Comparisons and benchmarks are identified and selected against "best-in-class" academic and operational processes to ensure that the institution is setting stretch targets and goals within its strategic planning process.*

- *Institution conducts comparisons and benchmarks to improve program and service delivery, cycle-time reduction of internal operations, and improved support services to students and other customers.*

 Approach   ☑ Deployment   ☐ Results

2.2a   Institution's criteria and rationale for comparisons and benchmarks to help drive improvement in academic and operational performance.

+ Strengths

1.

2.

3.

- Opportunities for Improvement

1.

2.

3.

Strategic Planning Issues:

    Short Term (1 to 2 years)

      1.

      2.

    Long Term (2 years or more)

      1.

      2.

2.2b   Do you evaluate the scope and validity of your comparison and benchmark process to improve planning and overall performance?

Notes for application writing:

Zero-Based   **World-Class**

0	10	20	30	40	50	60	70	80	90	100

(Circle Appropriate Percentile)

Zero-Based Institution

- *Institution has no documented plan to evaluate and improve the scope, sources, and uses of comparison and benchmark data.*

- *Institution places no value on comparisons and benchmarks against other educational providers or other institutions.*

- *Benchmarking is not used to set "stretch" goals and to improve critical academic and operational processes.*

World-Class Institution

- *Institution has published a document that outlines how to conduct comparisons and benchmarks against other educational providers and organizations.*

- *Benchmarking activities are strategically driven from student and other customer surveys.*

- *Comparisons and benchmarking data are reviewed and evaluated quarterly to improve institutional planning and overall performance.*

☑ Approach   ☑ Deployment   ☐ Results

2.2b   Institution's evaluation and improvement of its comparison and benchmark process.

+ Strengths

1.

2.

3.

- Opportunities for Improvement

1.

2.

3.

Strategic Planning Issues:

    Short Term (1 to 2 years)

      1.

      2.

    Long Term (2 years or more)

      1.

      2.

2.3 NOTES

2.3 Analysis and Use of Institution-Level Data (35 points)

Describe how data related to educational progress and business operational performance are analyzed to support institution-level review, action, and planning.

AREAS TO ADDRESS

a. how information and data from all parts of the institution are integrated and analyzed to support education-related reviews, decisions, and planning. Describe how analysis is used to gain understanding of: (1) student and group performance; (2) school program performance; and (3) comparative performance of students, student groups, and school programs.

b. how information and data from all parts of the institution are integrated and analyzed to support business operations-related reviews, decisions, and planning. Describe how analysis is used to gain understanding of: (1) institutional business operational performance; and (2) institutional business operational performance relative to appropriately selected organizations.

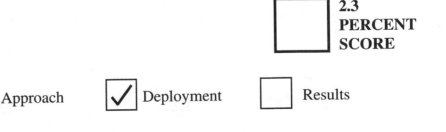

2.3 PERCENT SCORE

☑ Approach   ☑ Deployment   ☐ Results

2.3a   Does your institution systematically integrate and analyze data from all areas of the institution to support academic planning and improved student performance?

Notes for application writing:

Zero-Based   World-Class

| 0 | 10 | 20 | 30 | 40 | 50 | 60 | 70 | 80 | 90 | 100 |

(Circle Appropriate Percentile)

Zero-Based Institution

- *Institution does not analyze data to support academic planning and improved performance.*

- *No evidence exists that the institution collects financial, student, and operational performance data and translates it into information for faculty and staff to use to improve student service and operational performance.*

- *Student and other customer data analyses are not systematically linked to key quality indicators established within the institution.*

World-Class Institution

- *Institution collects student retention, satisfaction, and class performance data before developing a new curriculum schedule for the school of business.*

- *Institution uses institution-wide student food satisfaction survey results and financial results from food service department before developing new menus for the cafeteria.*

- *Each department focuses on selected quality indicators for faculty (e.g., timeliness of student feedback, accuracy of reports back to students, cycle-time improvement of student report cards, and student satisfaction.)*

 ✓ Approach   ✓ Deployment   ☐ Results

2.3a   Institution's integration and analysis of data to support academic planning and improved student performance.

+ Strengths

1.

2.

3.

- Opportunities for Improvement

1.

2.

3.

Strategic Planning Issues:

Short Term (1 to 2 years)

1.

2.

Long Term (2 years or more)

1.

2.

2.3b   Does your institution systematically integrate and analyze data from all areas of the institution to support operational planning and improved operational performance?

Notes for application writing:

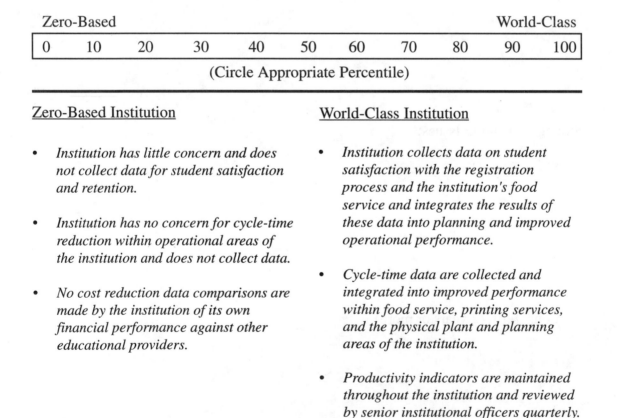

Zero-Based   World-Class

| 0 | 10 | 20 | 30 | 40 | 50 | 60 | 70 | 80 | 90 | 100 |

(Circle Appropriate Percentile)

Zero-Based Institution

- *Institution has little concern and does not collect data for student satisfaction and retention.*

- *Institution has no concern for cycle-time reduction within operational areas of the institution and does not collect data.*

- *No cost reduction data comparisons are made by the institution of its own financial performance against other educational providers.*

World-Class Institution

- *Institution collects data on student satisfaction with the registration process and the institution's food service and integrates the results of these data into planning and improved operational performance.*

- *Cycle-time data are collected and integrated into improved performance within food service, printing services, and the physical plant and planning areas of the institution.*

- *Productivity indicators are maintained throughout the institution and reviewed by senior institutional officers quarterly.*

☑ Approach   ☑ Deployment   ☐ Results

2.3b   Institution's integration and analysis of data from all areas to support operational planning and improved operational performance.

+ Strengths

1.

2.

3.

- Opportunities for Improvement

1.

2.

3.

Strategic Planning Issues:

Short Term (1 to 2 years)

1.

2.

Long Term (2 years or more)

1.

2.

CHAPTER FIVE

Category 3.0
Strategic and
Operational Planning_____

3.0 Strategic and Operational Planning (75 points)[8]

The Strategic and Operational Planning Category examines how the institution sets strategic directions, and how it determines key plan requirements. Also examined is how the plan requirements are translated into an effective performance management system, with a primary focus on student performance.

---

[8] Source: Strategic Quality Planning Category 3.0 Criteria has been rewritten and revised for institutions of higher education and simplified based on the 1995 Malcolm Baldrige National Quality Award Education Pilot Criteria.

3.1 Strategy Development (45 points)

Describe the institution's planning process and how this process determines and addresses key student and overall school performance requirements. Describe also how this process focuses on student and overall institutional performance improvement and includes an effective basis for the implementation of plans and the evaluation of progress relative to plans.

AREAS TO ADDRESS

a. how the institution develops strategies and plans to address key student and institution performance requirements focusing on improved student and overall institutional performance. Describe how strategy development addresses: (1) student needs and expectations; (2) key external factors, requirements, and opportunities; (3) key internal factors, including involvement of the institution's units; and (4) improvement of student and overall institutional performance.

b. how strategies and plans are translated into critical success factors and deployed to institutional units.

c. how the institution evaluates and improves its strategic planning and plan-deployment processes, including the improvement of planning completion time and deployment time.

3.1
PERCENT
SCORE

 ✓ Approach   ✓ Deployment   ☐ Results

3.1a   How is your institution's overall planning process addressing student and institutional performance improvement?

Notes for application writing:

Zero-Based   World-Class

0	10	20	30	40	50	60	70	80	90	100

(Circle Appropriate Percentile)

Zero-Based Institution

- *Institution's strategic plan does not address key student and institutional performance.*

- *No evidence exists that institution considers new courses and program offerings when developing their long-term strategic plan.*

- *Institution does not integrate improved cycle time with student/customer focus and operational performance in its planning process.*

World-Class Institution

- *Each division throughout the institution develops goals to support short- and long-term objectives that address student and overall institutional performance.*

- *Faculty, staff, and students are involved in both short- and long-term planning within each division throughout the institution.*

- *New enrollment requirements are considered when developing strategies and plans for key student and institutional programs.*

☑ Approach   ☑ Deployment   ☐ Results

3.1a   Institution's plans and strategies address key student and institutional performance improvement.

+ Strengths

1.

2.

3.

- Opportunities for Improvement

1.

2.

3.

Strategic Planning Issues:

Short Term (1 to 2 years)

1.

2.

Long Term (2 years or more)

1.

2.

3.1b   Are your institution's strategic plans deployed throughout the institution and translated into actionable initiatives?

Notes for application writing:

Zero-Based   World-Class

0	10	20	30	40	50	60	70	80	90	100

(Circle Appropriate Percentile)

Zero-Based Institution

- *Institution does not share strategic plans beyond senior institutional officer level.*

- *Institution's strategic plan is anecdotal and only known by senior administration.*

- *Strategic plan is shared throughout the institution, but no actionable initiatives are incorporated within each division.*

World-Class Institution

- *Institution shares strategic plan throughout the institution and requires that actionable initiatives be developed within each division.*

- *Quarterly reviews are conducted within each division to check division progress against the institution's strategic plan.*

- *Institution shares strategic plan with all students, faculty, and staff and requests input before developing actionable initiatives.*

 ✓ Approach   ✓ Deployment   ☐ Results

3.1b   Strategic plans deployed and translated into actionable initiatives throughout the institution.

+ Strengths

1.

2.

3.

- Opportunities for Improvement

1.

2.

3.

Strategic Planning Issues:

Short Term (1 to 2 years)

1.

2.

Long Term (2 years or more)

1.

2.

3.1c   Are your institution's strategic plans evaluated and deployed throughout the institution?

Notes for application writing:

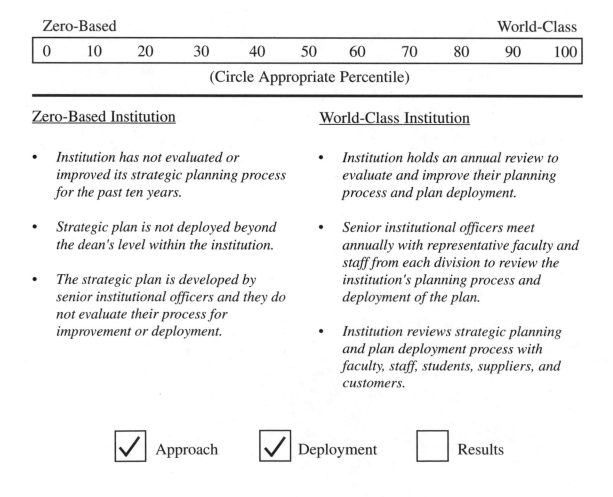

Zero-Based   World-Class

| 0 | 10 | 20 | 30 | 40 | 50 | 60 | 70 | 80 | 90 | 100 |

(Circle Appropriate Percentile)

Zero-Based Institution

- *Institution has not evaluated or improved its strategic planning process for the past ten years.*

- *Strategic plan is not deployed beyond the dean's level within the institution.*

- *The strategic plan is developed by senior institutional officers and they do not evaluate their process for improvement or deployment.*

World-Class Institution

- *Institution holds an annual review to evaluate and improve their planning process and plan deployment.*

- *Senior institutional officers meet annually with representative faculty and staff from each division to review the institution's planning process and deployment of the plan.*

- *Institution reviews strategic planning and plan deployment process with faculty, staff, students, suppliers, and customers.*

☑ Approach   ☑ Deployment   ☐ Results

3.1c   Strategic plans evaluated and deployed throughout the institution.

+ Strengths

1.

2.

3.

- Opportunities for Improvement

1.

2.

3.

Strategic Planning Issues:

Short Term (1 to 2 years)

1.

2.

Long Term (2 years or more)

1.

2.

3.2 NOTES

3.2 Strategy Deployment (30 points)

Summarize the institution's critical success factors and how they are deployed. Show how the institution's performance projects into the future.

AREAS TO ADDRESS

a. summary of the specific critical success factors derived from the institution's plan and how these factors are translated into an action plan. Describe: (1) key objectives and requirements, associated measures and/or indicators and how they are deployed; (2) how the plans address cooperation among units that contribute to the same plan elements; (3) how student performance and faculty and staff productivity are addressed in plans and targets; and (4) the principal resources committed to the accomplishment of plans.

b. two-to-five-year projection of key measures and/or indicators of the institution's student performance and business operational performance. Briefly describe how student-related and business operational performance might be expected to compare with: (1) the institution's past performance; (2) comparable institutions; and (3) key benchmarks. Briefly explain the comparisons, including any estimates or assumptions made regarding comparable institutions and benchmarks.

3.2
PERCENT
SCORE

 Approach    Deployment   ☐ Results

3.2a   Does your institution have improvement and performance goals and strategies in place and are they translated into actionable requirements for all divisions?

Notes for application writing:

Zero-Based   World-Class

| 0 | 10 | 20 | 30 | 40 | 50 | 60 | 70 | 80 | 90 | 100 |

(Circle Appropriate Percentile)

Zero-Based Institution

- *No evidence exists that short- and long-term goals and strategies have been established by the institution.*

- *Institution has long-term goals and strategies developed, but has not deployed nor developed actionable requirements for each division.*

- *No alignment exists between the institution's short- and long-term goals and strategies and each division's operational performance.*

World-Class Institution

- *Each division has in place actionable performance goals and strategies that are fully integrated with the institution's short- and long-term strategic plans.*

- *Each department head receives a quarterly updated progress report toward meeting his division's short-term goals against the institution's long-term goals.*

- *Both short- and long-term goals and strategies and actionable progress is shared with faculty, staff, and students by each dean within the institution.*

 ✓ Approach   ✓ Deployment   ☐ Results

3.2a Institution has performance goals and strategies with actionable requirements for all divisions.

+ Strengths

1.

2.

3.

- Opportunities for Improvement

1.

2.

3.

Strategic Planning Issues:

Short Term (1 to 2 years)

1.

2.

Long Term (2 years or more)

1.

2.

3.2b   Explain how your institution's two-to-five-year projections of key measures are improving student achievement and operational performance.

Notes for application writing:

Zero-Based   World-Class

0	10	20	30	40	50	60	70	80	90	100

(Circle Appropriate Percentile)

Zero-Based Institution

- *Institution's projections for future performance are not based on comparisons or benchmarks.*

- *No projections of key measures are made by institution to improve student achievement or operational performance.*

- *Faculty and staff are not involved in making projections of key measures for student achievement.*

World-Class Institution

- *Faculty and staff are involved in making long-term projections for improved student achievement and operational performance within the institution.*

- *Long-term projections are shared with all faculty and staff after their input has been received.*

- *Institution's long-term projections are based on comparisons, benchmarks, and institution-wide input.*

☑ Approach   ☑ Deployment   ☐ Results

3.2b   Institution's projections of key measures have improved student achievement and operational performance.

+ Strengths

1.

2.

3.

- Opportunities for Improvement

1.

2.

3.

Strategic Planning Issues:

   Short Term (1 to 2 years)

     1.

     2.

   Long Term (2 years or more)

     1.

     2.

CHAPTER SIX

Category 4.0
Human Resource
Development and
Management _____

4.0 Human Resource Development and Management (150 points)[9]

The Human Resource Development and Management Category examines how faculty and staff development are aligned with the institution's performance objectives. Also examined are the institution's efforts to build and maintain a climate conducive to performance excellence, full participation, and personal and organizational growth.

---

[9] Source: Human Resource Development and Management Category 4.0 has been rewritten and revised for institutions of higher education and simplified based on the 1995 Malcolm Baldrige National Quality Award Education Pilot Criteria.

4.1 NOTES

4.1 Human Resource Planning and Evaluation (30 points)

Describe how the institution's human resource planning and evaluation are aligned with the institution's overall performance improvement plans and address the development and well-being of faculty and staff.

AREAS TO ADDRESS

a. how the institution translates overall performance requirement from planning (Category 3.0) to specific human resource plans. Summarize key plans in the following areas: (1) faculty and staff preparation and development; (2) faculty and staff recruitment, including expected or planned changes in demographic makeup of faculty and staff; (3) promotion, compensation, and benefits; and (4) expectation of faculty and academic units. For (1) through (4), distinguish between the short term and the long term, and segment by employee category, as appropriate.

b. how the institution evaluates and improves its human resource planning and the alignment of human resource plans with overall plans. Include how faculty and staff-related data and institution performance data are analyzed and used: (1) to assess the development and well-being of all categories and types of faculty and staff; (2) to assess the linkage of human resource practices with key performance results; and (3) to ensure that reliable and complete human resource information is available for planning.

4.1 PERCENT SCORE

 Approach    Deployment   ☐ Results

4.1a   Are your institution's human resource plans driven by the goals outlined in your overall plan (e.g., faculty/staff recruitment, faculty/staff develoment, training, empowerment, and recognition)?

Notes for application writing:

Zero-Based   World-Class

0	10	20	30	40	50	60	70	80	90	100

(Circle Appropriate Percentile)

Zero-Based Institution

- *Performance evaluations for faculty and staff not written in language that reinforces the institution's values.*

- *Training widely dispersed but not focused for faculty/staff member individual career development within the institution.*

- *Institution does not have in place a recognition program for faculty and staff that is strategically aligned with the institution's short- and long-term plans and goals.*

World-Class Institution

- *Human resource plans integrated with the institution's short- and long-term strategic plan.*

- *Institution reflects a team culture and supports this concept through its faculty and staff development programs.*

- *Faculty and staff are recognized for meeting and exceeding the institution's strategic plans and goals within their divisions.*

☑ Approach   ☑ Deployment   ☐ Results

4.1a   Institution's human resource plans.

+ Strengths

1.

2.

3.

- Opportunities for Improvement

1.

2.

3.

Strategic Planning Issues:

    Short Term (1 to 2 years)

       1.

       2.

    Long Term (2 years or more)

       1.

       2.

4.1b   Does your institution evaluate and improve the alignment of its human resource planning with its overall plans?

Notes for application writing:

Zero-Based   World-Class

0	10	20	30	40	50	60	70	80	90	100

(Circle Appropriate Percentile)

Zero-Based Institution

- *No process in place for recruitment and hiring of new faculty and staff that is reflective of the institution's quality culture.*

- *Institution does not align their human resource plan with its overall strategic plan.*

- *Human resource management does not appear to be driven by the institution's overall plan.*

World-Class Institution

- *Institution publishes an employee newsletter that communicates values and student/customer focus, which is aligned with the institution's overall plan.*

- *Institution conducts a faculty/staff satisfaction survey to gauge employee satisfaction.*

- *Faculty and staff are categorized by rank and position, and career development plans and training are developed for each employee category.*

☑ Approach   ☑ Deployment   ☐ Results

4.1b   Institution's alignment of human resource plan with overall plans.

+ Strengths

1.

2.

3.

- Opportunities for Improvement

1.

2.

3.

Strategic Planning Issues:

Short Term (1 to 2 years)

1.

2.

Long Term (2 years or more)

1.

2.

4.2 NOTES

4.2 Faculty and Staff Work Systems (30 points)

Describe how the institution's faculty and staff position responsibilities promote a student focus, cross-functional cooperation, and high performance. Describe also how evaluation, compensation, promotion, and recognition reinforce these objectives.

AREAS TO ADDRESS

a. how faculty responsibilities promote a focus on student performance improvement. Describe how the responsibilities: (1) ensure effective communications and cooperation across functions or units that need to work together to meet student and institution educational requirements; and (2) are reinforced by the institution's approach to evaluation, compensation, promotion, and recognition.

b. how the institution's work and job design promote high staff performance. Describe how work and job design: (1) create opportunities for initiative and self-directed responsibility; (2) foster flexibility and rapid response to changing requirements; (3) ensure effective communications and cooperation across functions or units that need to work together to meet student and/or business operational requirements; and (4) are reinforced by the institution's approach to evaluation, compensation, promotion, and recognition.

**4.2
PERCENT
SCORE**

 Approach    Deployment   ☐ Results

4.2a   How does your institution's faculty promote a student and customer focus?

Notes for application writing:

Zero-Based   World-Class

| 0 | 10 | 20 | 30 | 40 | 50 | 60 | 70 | 80 | 90 | 100 |

(Circle Appropriate Percentile)

Zero-Based Institution

- *Faculty does not promote a focus on student performance improvement.*

- *Faculty members are not recognized or rewarded for promoting a student and customer focus.*

- *Faculty members do not work together to promote a student-focused environment within the institution.*

World-Class Institution

- *Special recognition awards given to faculty members who promote a student and customer focus.*

- *President's Club award in place to promote faculty and staff contributions to student performance improvement.*

- *Faculty and staff cross-functional team in place to promote a better student and other customer focus among divisions.*

☑ Approach   ☑ Deployment   ☐ Results

4.2a   Faculty's promotion of student and customer focus.

+ Strengths

1.

2.

3.

Opportunities for Improvement

1.

2.

3

Strategic Planning Issues:

   Short Term (1 to 2 years)

      1.

      2.

   Long Term (2 years or more)

      1.

      2.

4.2b   Does your institution give staff the authority or autonomy to solve problems and make decisions within their work areas?

Notes for application writing:

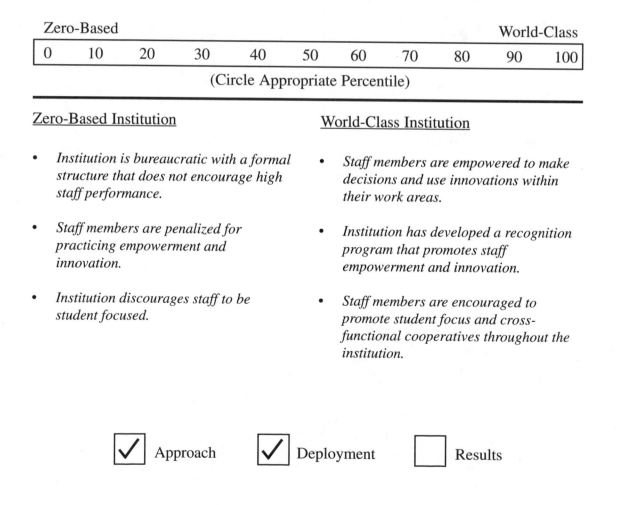

Zero-Based   World-Class

| 0 | 10 | 20 | 30 | 40 | 50 | 60 | 70 | 80 | 90 | 100 |

(Circle Appropriate Percentile)

Zero-Based Institution

- *Institution is bureaucratic with a formal structure that does not encourage high staff performance.*

- *Staff members are penalized for practicing empowerment and innovation.*

- *Institution discourages staff to be student focused.*

World-Class Institution

- *Staff members are empowered to make decisions and use innovations within their work areas.*

- *Institution has developed a recognition program that promotes staff empowerment and innovation.*

- *Staff members are encouraged to promote student focus and cross-functional cooperatives throughout the institution.*

☑ Approach   ☑ Deployment   ☐ Results

4.2b   Institution's promotion of high performance and self-directed responsibilities among staff.

\+ Strengths

1.

2.

3.

\- Opportunities for Improvement

1.

2.

3.

Strategic Planning Issues:

Short Term (1 to 2 years)

1.

2.

Long Term (2 years or more)

1.

2.

4.3 NOTES

4.3 Faculty and Staff Development (50 points)

Describe how the institution's faculty and staff development advances the institution's plans and contributes to faculty and staff performance improvement, development, and advancement.

AREAS TO ADDRESS

a. how the institution encourages and enables faculty to meet institution and personal objectives. Describe how each of the following is addressed. (1) orientation of new faculty regarding key plans and expectations; (2) workshops, classes, and training programs for all faculty addressing key performance requirements; and (3) how the institution evaluates the effectiveness of faculty development efforts.

b. how the institution's staff education and training are designed, delivered, reinforced, and evaluated. Include: (1) how employees and supervisors work together in determining specific education and training needs and designing education and training; (2) how education and training are delivered; (3) how knowledge and skills are reinforced through on-the-job application; and (4) how education and training are evaluated and improved to achieve institutional and personal objectives.

4.3 PERCENT SCORE

 Approach 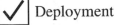 Deployment ☐ Results

4.3a   How does your institution encourage and enable faculty to meet institutional and personal goals and objectives (e.g., orientation of new faculty, workshops, classes, training programs, student and peer review, etc.)?

Notes for application writing:

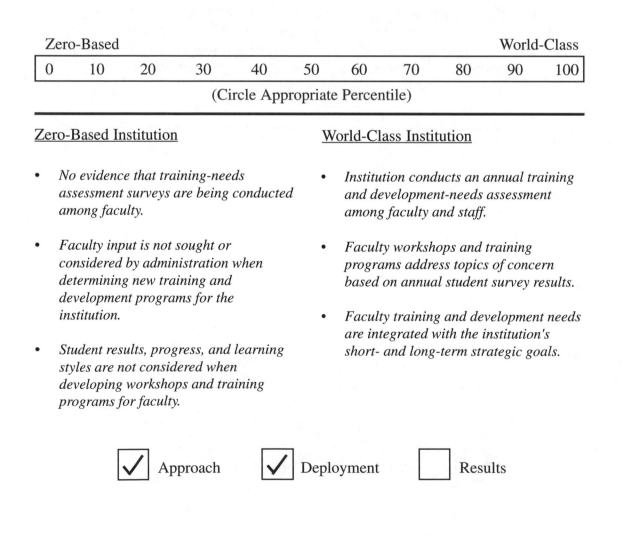

Zero-Based   World-Class

| 0 | 10 | 20 | 30 | 40 | 50 | 60 | 70 | 80 | 90 | 100 |

(Circle Appropriate Percentile)

Zero-Based Institution

- *No evidence that training-needs assessment surveys are being conducted among faculty.*

- *Faculty input is not sought or considered by administration when determining new training and development programs for the institution.*

- *Student results, progress, and learning styles are not considered when developing workshops and training programs for faculty.*

World-Class Institution

- *Institution conducts an annual training and development-needs assessment among faculty and staff.*

- *Faculty workshops and training programs address topics of concern based on annual student survey results.*

- *Faculty training and development needs are integrated with the institution's short- and long-term strategic goals.*

☑ Approach   ☑ Deployment   ☐ Results

4.3a   Institution encourages and enables faculty to meet institutional and personal goals and objectives.

+ Strengths

1.

2.

3.

- Opportunities for Improvement

1.

2.

3.

Strategic Planning Issues:

   Short Term (1 to 2 years)

      1.

      2.

   Long Term (2 years or more)

      1.

      2.

4.3b   How does your institution design, deliver, reinforce, and evaluate education and training that is delivered to staff?

Notes for application writing:

Zero-Based   World-Class

0	10	20	30	40	50	60	70	80	90	100

(Circle Appropriate Percentile)

Zero-Based Institution

- *Staff has no input into the types of training that is offered.*

- *Education and training are delivered to staff one time per year using only the lecture method of instruction.*

- *Staff knowledge and skills learned in various education and training courses are not reinforced and applied on the job.*

World-Class Institution

- *Staff training throughout the institution reflects the institution's strategic goals and objectives.*

- *Staff members are encouraged to complete assessments after each workshop, class, and training program to evaluate and comment on future improvement.*

- *Staff members are assessed after receiving training on how they apply new knowledge to on-the-job improvement.*

☑ Approach   ☑ Deployment   ☐ Results

4.3b   Institution has in place education and training for staff.

+ Strengths

1.

2.

3.

- Opportunities for Improvement

1.

2.

3.

Strategic Planning Issues:

    Short Term (1 to 2 years)

      1.

      2.

    Long Term (2 years or more)

      1.

      2.

4.4 NOTES

4.4 Faculty and Staff Well-Being and Satisfaction (40 points)

Describe how the institution maintains a work environment and a work climate conducive to the well-being and satisfaction of faculty and staff and focused on the institution's performance objectives.

AREAS TO ADDRESS

a. how the institution maintains a safe and healthful work environment. Describe: (1) how faculty and staff well-being factors such as health, safety, and ergonomics are included in improvement activities; and (2) for each factor relevant and important to the institution's work environment, principal performance improvement requirements, measures and/or indicators, and targets. Note significant differences based upon differences in work environments or special requirements among faculty and staff categories or units.

b. what services, facilities, activities, and opportunities the institution makes available to faculty and staff to support their overall well-being and satisfaction and/or enhance their work experience and development potential.

c. how the institution determines faculty and staff satisfaction, well-being, and motivation. Include a brief description of methods, frequency, the specific factors used in this determination, and how the information is used to improve satisfaction, well-being, and motivation. Note any important differences in methods or factors used for different groups or types of employees, as appropriate.

**4.4
PERCENT
SCORE**

 Approach   ☑ Deployment   ☐ Results

4.4a   Does your institution work on projects to improve safety, health, ergonomics, faculty/staff morale, and work force satisfaction?

Notes for application writing:

Zero-Based   World-Class

0	10	20	30	40	50	60	70	80	90	100

(Circle Appropriate Percentile)

Zero-Based Institution

- *No specific department or individual is dedicated to faculty/staff safety and ergonomics issues within the institution.*

- *Senior institutional officers are unaware of employee morale issues.*

- *No faculty/staff surveys or focus groups are conducted to determine well-being and satisfaction.*

World-Class Institution

- *Faculty and staff health issues are viewed as of paramount importance to the institution.*

- *Personal counseling is available for faculty and staff.*

- *Institution conducts annual faculty/staff surveys and focus groups to determine well-being and satisfaction. On the basis of survey results, the institution has established quality indicators to gauge improvement.*

[✓] Approach   [✓] Deployment   [ ] Results

4.4a   Well-being and morale of faculty and staff.

+ Strengths

1.

2.

3.

- Opportunities for Improvement

1.

2.

3.

Strategic Planning Issues:

Short Term (1 to 2 years)

1.

2.

Long Term (2 years or more)

1.

2.

4.4b   What services, facilities, activities, and opportunities does your institution offer to support the overall well-being and morale of faculty/staff?

Notes for application writing:

Zero-Based   World-Class

0	10	20	30	40	50	60	70	80	90	100

(Circle Appropriate Percentile)

Zero-Based Institution

- *No evidence exists that the institution uses a survey process to improve its faculty/staff well-being and satisfaction.*

- *Institution has limited recreational and cultural acitivies for faculty/staff.*

- *Institution offers very limited special services for faculty and staff.*

World-Class Institution

- *Faculty/staff focus groups are conducted quarterly within each division to discuss work force issues.*

- *Institution has developed flexible work hours for staff and special outplacement services for faculty and staff.*

- *Institution provides special services for faculty and staff that include: day care, special leave for community services, career enhancement activities, and career counseling.*

☑ Approach   ☑ Deployment   ☐ Results

4.4b   Services offered by institution that support well-being and morale of faculty/staff.

+ Strengths

1.

2.

3.

Opportunities for Improvement

1.

2.

3.

Strategic Planning Issues:

Short Term (1 to 2 years)

1.

2.

Long Term (2 years or more)

1.

2.

4.4c   How does your institution determine faculty and staff satisfaction (e.g., surveys, faculty/staff focus groups, etc.)?

Notes for application writing:

Zero-Based   World-Class

0	10	20	30	40	50	60	70	80	90	100

(Circle Appropriate Percentile)

Zero-Based Institution   World-Class Institution

- *No evidence that a process is in place to determine faculty/staff satisfaction.*

- *No benchmarks are conducted to compare institution's faculty/staff satisfaction data with those of other educational providers or outside organizations.*

- *Faculty/staff satisfaction and well-being data are not considered within institution's planning proess.*

- *Annual faculty/staff satisfaction survey conducted.*

- *Faculty/staff focus groups are deployed throughout the institution to discuss and determine satisfaction and well-being issues.*

- *Faculty/staff satisfaction and morale survey data are integrated into the institution's planning process.*

☑ Approach   ☑ Deployment   ☐ Results

4.4c   Institution's method for determining faculty and staff satisfaction.

+ Strengths

1.

2.

3.

- Opportunities for Improvement

1.

2.

3.

Strategic Planning Issues:

   Short Term (1 to 2 years)

   1.

   2.

   Long Term (2 years or more)

   1.

   2.

CHAPTER SEVEN

Category 5.0
Educational and Business
Process Management _____

5.0 Educational and Business Process Management (150 points)[10]

The Educational and Business Process Management Category examines the key aspects of process management, including learning-focused education design, education delivery, institutional services, and business operations. The Category examines how key processes are designed, effectively managed, and improved to achieve higher performance.

---

[10] Source: Management of Process Quality Category 5.0 has been rewritten and revised for institutions of higher education and simplified based on the 1995 Malcolm Baldrige National Quality Award Education Pilot Criteria.

5.1 Education Design (40 points)

Describe how new and/or modified educational programs and offerings are designed and introduced.

AREAS TO ADDRESS

a. how educational programs and offerings are designed. Describe how the institution ensures that: (1) all programs and offerings address student needs and meet high standards; (2) sequencing and offering linkages are appropriately considered; (3) a measurement plan is in place; and (4) faculty are properly prepared.

b. how design takes into account educational program and offering delivery. Describe how the institution ensures that all educational programs and offerings: (1) focus on active learning, anticipating and preparing for individual differences in student learning rates and styles; (2) make effective use of formative and summative assessment; (3) have adequate faculty-student contact, and (4) include appropriate formative and summative feedback mechanisms.

c. how the institution evaluates and improves its design of educational programs and offerings. Describe: (1) the factors and information used in the evaluation; and (2) the frequency and content of evaluations and who conducts the evaluation.

5.1
PERCENT
SCORE

 Approach    Deployment   ☐ Results

5.1a   Does your institution employ a systematic process that addresses and translates student and other customer needs into new or modified program characteristics and standards?

Notes for application writing:

Zero-Based										World-Class
0	10	20	30	40	50	60	70	80	90	100

(Circle Appropriate Percentile)

Zero-Based Institution

- *No process in place to determine student and other customer requirements.*

- *Design of new programs and services are not based on student input.*

- *No measurement plan for new programs is developed, nor is faculty updated and trained on program changes before the semester begins.*

World-Class Institution

- *Surveys used to determine student and other program needs.*

- *Student satisfaction is measured each semester on all new programs.*

- *Faculty members are updated and trained within each department on all new programs and institutional offerings.*

 ✓ Approach   ✓ Deployment   ☐ Results

5.1a   Institution's translation of student and other customer requirements and needs into a newer modified program design.

+ Strengths

1.

2.

3.

- Opportunities for Improvement

1.

2.

3.

Strategic Planning Issues:

　Short Term (1 to 2 years)

　　1.

　　2.

　Long Term (2 years or more)

　　1.

　　2.

5.1b   Describe the overall process your institution uses to design and test new and/or modified programs and services.

Notes for application writing:

Zero-Based   World-Class

0	10	20	30	40	50	60	70	80	90	100

(Circle Appropriate Percentile)

Zero-Based Institution

- *No consideration is given to individual differences in student learning rates and styles when designing new programs or modifying existing offerings.*

- *No learning assessment process is in place to help determine how to modify program offerings within the institution.*

- *No refined, documented research approach institution-wide is in place to assure consistency in program design plans and testing before introduction of new programs and/or program modifications.*

World-Class Institution

- *Documented program design qualifications and release procedures are in place to test new programs and/or modification of existing programs.*

- *All new program and service designs are reviewed and validated by a cross-discipline faculty team.*

- *All program feedback is incorporated into design change before introduction within the institution.*

 ☑ Approach   ☑ Deployment   ☐ Results

5.1b   Institution's review and validation of new and/or modified programs and service designs.

+ Strengths

1.

2.

3.

- Opportunities for Improvement

1.

2.

3.

Strategic Planning Issues:

  Short Term (1 to 2 years)

  1.

  2.

  Long Term (2 years or more)

  1.

  2.

5.1c   Does your institution systematically evaluate and improve its design of new and/or modified programs and offerings?

Notes for application writing:

Zero-Based   World-Class

0	10	20	30	40	50	60	70	80	90	100

(Circle Appropriate Percentile)

Zero-Based Institution

- *No documented procedure for continuously improving programs and services is in place.*

- *Program and service designs and design processes are not evaluated for improvement.*

- *New programs are evaluated once every five years, but few changes are made as a result of the evaluation.*

World-Class Institution

- *Institution evaluates programs and offerings semiannually.*

- *New programs are evaluated annually by a cross-functional team of faculty, staff, and students.*

- *Institution changes program design based on student and faculty input each semester.*

 ✓ Approach   ✓ Deployment   ☐ Results

5.1c   Institution's evaluation and improvement of program design.

+ Strengths

1.

2.

3.

- Opportunities for Improvement

1.

2.

3.

Strategic Planning Issues:

    Short Term (1 to 2 years)

       1.

       2.

    Long Term (2 years or more)

       1.

       2.

5.2 NOTES

5.2 Education Delivery (25 points)

Describe how the institution ensures that delivery of educational programs and offerings meets the design requirements.

AREAS TO ADDRESS

a. how the institution ensures that ongoing academic programs and offerings meet the design requirements addressed in Item 5.1. Describe: (1) what observations, measures, and/or indicators are used and who uses them; and (2) how the observations, measures, and/or indicators are used to provide timely information to help students and faculty.

b. how academic programs and offerings are evaluated and improved. Describe how each of the following is used or considered: (1) information from students and/or families; (2) benchmarking best practices in education and other fields; (3) use of assessment results; (4) peer evaluation; (5) research on learning, assessment, and faculty presentation; (6) information from employers and governing bodies; and (7) use of technology.

5.2 PERCENT SCORE

 Approach    Deployment   ☐ Results

5.2a   How does your institution ensure that programs and offerings meet design requirements?

Notes for application writing:

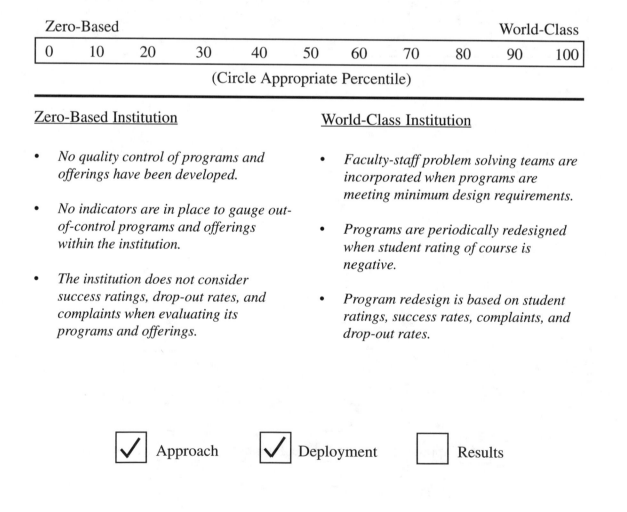

Zero-Based   World-Class

| 0 | 10 | 20 | 30 | 40 | 50 | 60 | 70 | 80 | 90 | 100 |

(Circle Appropriate Percentile)

Zero-Based Institution

- *No quality control of programs and offerings have been developed.*

- *No indicators are in place to gauge out-of-control programs and offerings within the institution.*

- *The institution does not consider success ratings, drop-out rates, and complaints when evaluating its programs and offerings.*

World-Class Institution

- *Faculty-staff problem solving teams are incorporated when programs are meeting minimum design requirements.*

- *Programs are periodically redesigned when student rating of course is negative.*

- *Program redesign is based on student ratings, success rates, complaints, and drop-out rates.*

☑ Approach   ☑ Deployment   ☐ Results

5.2a   Institution's programs and offerings meet design requirements.

+ Strengths

1.

2.

3.

- Opportunities for Improvement

1.

2.

3.

Strategic Planning Issues:

   Short Term (1 to 2 years)

    1.

    2.

   Long Term (2 years or more)

    1.

    2.

5.2b   How does your institution evaluate and improve its academic programs and offerings?

Notes for application writing:

Zero-Based   World-Class

| 0 | 10 | 20 | 30 | 40 | 50 | 60 | 70 | 80 | 90 | 100 |

(Circle Appropriate Percentile)

Zero-Based Institution

- *Institution does not use a systematic approach to evaluate critical processes to ensure that its academic programs and offerings meet design requirements.*

- *No evidence that institution evaluates its academic programs and offerings.*

- *Institution does not consider attendance, drop-out rates, complaints, and student feedback to improve its programs*

World-Class Institution

- *Institution uses a structured evaluation process to ensure that its academic programs and offerings meet design requirements.*

- *Institution incorporates simple flowcharting of key programs to achieve better program and service delivery and shortened cycle time.*

- *Institution benchmarks other institutions and organizations to evaluate and improve its academic programs and offerings.*

☑ Approach   ☑ Deployment   ☐ Results

5.2b   Institution evaluates and improves its programs and offerings.

+ Strengths

1.

2.

3.

- Opportunities for Improvement

1.

2.

3.

Strategic Planning Issues:

Short Term (1 to 2 years)

1.

2.

Long Term (2 years or more)

1.

2.

5.3 NOTES

5.3 Education Support Service Design and Delivery (25 points)

Describe how the institution's education support services are designed and managed to meet the needs of students and key stakeholders.

AREAS TO ADDRESS

a. how key education support services are selected and designed. Include: (1) how key requirements for each service are set, taking into account the needs of students and faculty; (2) how the key requirements are translated into effective operational requirements, including appropriate observations and/ or measurements; and (3) how the institution ensures that education support services are performing effectively.

b. how the education support services are evaluated and improved. Describe how each of the following is used or considered: (1) feedback from students and faculty; (2) benchmarking; (3) peer evaluation; and (4) data from observations and measurements.

5.3 PERCENT SCORE

 Approach   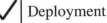 Deployment   ☐ Results

5.3a   How are key support services selected to meet the needs of students, faculty, staff, and key stakeholders?

Notes for application writing:

Zero-Based   World-Class

| 0 | 10 | 20 | 30 | 40 | 50 | 60 | 70 | 80 | 90 | 100 |

(Circle Appropriate Percentile)

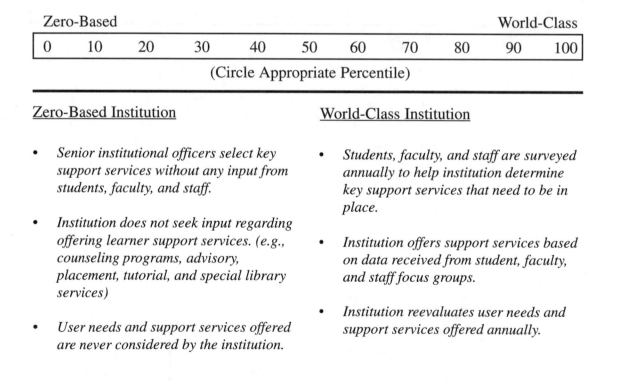

Zero-Based Institution

- *Senior institutional officers select key support services without any input from students, faculty, and staff.*

- *Institution does not seek input regarding offering learner support services. (e.g., counseling programs, advisory, placement, tutorial, and special library services)*

- *User needs and support services offered are never considered by the institution.*

World-Class Institution

- *Students, faculty, and staff are surveyed annually to help institution determine key support services that need to be in place.*

- *Institution offers support services based on data received from student, faculty, and staff focus groups.*

- *Institution reevaluates user needs and support services offered annually.*

☑ Approach   ☑ Deployment   ☐ Results

5.3a   Key support services selected.

+ Strengths

1.

2.

3.

- Opportunities for Improvement

1.

2.

3.

Strategic Planning Issues:

Short Term (1 to 2 years)

1.

2.

Long Term (2 years or more)

1.

2.

5.3b   Does your institution evaluate and improve support services on an ongoing basis?

Notes for application writing:

Zero-Based   World-Class

| 0 | 10 | 20 | 30 | 40 | 50 | 60 | 70 | 80 | 90 | 100 |

(Circle Appropriate Percentile)

Zero-Based Institution

- *Institution does not evaluate support services.*

- *Support services are changed based on user complaints. No considerations are given to impact on institution's total programs and offerings.*

- *Institution does not compare or benchmark other institutions' support services which are considered to be best-in-class.*

World-Class Institution

- *Institution conducts benchmarks on a regular basis to identify improvement opportunities within support services.*

- *Students and stakeholders are surveyed annually by the institution for input regarding shortened cycle time of various support services.*

- *Institution improves support services annually based on survey results.*

☑ Approach   ☑ Deployment   ☐ Results

5.3b   Institution's evaluation of support services.

+ Strengths

1.

2.

3.

- Opportunities for Improvement

1.

2.

3.

Strategic Planning Issues:

    Short Term (1 to 2 years)

       1.

       2.

    Long Term (2 years or more)

       1.

       2.

5.4 NOTES

5.4 Research, Scholarship, and Service (20 points)

Describe how the institution contributes to knowledge creation, knowledge transfer, and services via programs and activities. Describe also the benefits of these programs and activities to key communities and to the institution's mission objectives.

AREAS TO ADDRESS

a. how the institution contributes to knowledge creation and knowledge transfer to external communities. Describe: (1) key goals, target communities, and key measures and/or indicators of benefits; and (2) how the institution actively seeks to ensure the effective transfer of knowledge to key communities.

b. how research, scholarship, and service contribute to student learning, faculty development, and other key institutional mission objectives.

c. how research, scholarship, and service activities are evaluated and improved. Describe how each of the following is used or considered: (1) feedback from participants and beneficiaries; (2) peer evaluation; (3) data from observations and measurements; and (4) benchmarking information.

	5.4
	PERCENT
	SCORE

 ✔ Approach   ✔ Deployment   ☐ Results

5.4a   How does your institution create and transfer new learning and services to outside communities?

Notes for application writing:

Zero-Based   World-Class

0	10	20	30	40	50	60	70	80	90	100

(Circle Appropriate Percentile)

Zero-Based Institution

- *Institution does not partner with local organizations on research projects.*

- *Institution has no regard for transferring new knowledge and services to key communities in which they operate.*

- *Major research and service projects are not related to the institution's mission and are not transferred to external communities.*

World-Class Institution

- *Institution shares all new research with major organizations throughout the local community and state.*

- *Major institutional artistic activities are shared throughout the community with local cultural organizations.*

- *Faculty partners with businesses, social services, cultural organizations, and other organizations on most major research projects.*

☑ Approach   ☑ Deployment   ☐ Results

5.4a   Institution's transfer of new learning and services to outside communities.

+ Strengths

1.

2.

3.

- Opportunities for Improvement

1.

2.

3.

Strategic Planning Issues:

Short Term (1 to 2 years)

1.

2.

Long Term (2 years or more)

1.

2.

5.4b   How does your institution's research, scholarship, and services contribute to improved student, faculty, and staff performance and meet the institution's mission objectives?

Notes for application writing:

Zero-Based   World-Class

0	10	20	30	40	50	60	70	80	90	100

(Circle Appropriate Percentile)

Zero-Based Institution

- *Research, scholarship, and services are not connected with the institution's mission objectives.*

- *Institutional research does not contribute to student learning and faculty development.*

- *Institution is not concerned that its programs and activities have a limited relationship with improving student learning, faculty development, and other key mission objectives.*

World-Class Institution

- *Research is integrated with the institution's mission of promoting student learning.*

- *New programs are strategically developed to support the institution's key mission objectives.*

- *The school of education promotes research in faculty and staff development that supports one of the institution's key mission objectives.*

☑ Approach   ☑ Deployment   ☐ Results

5.4b   Institution's research, scholarship, and service contributions support improved performance and meet institutional mission objectives.

+ Strengths

1.

2.

3.

- Opportunities for Improvement

1.

2.

3.

Strategic Planning Issues:

Short Term (1 to 2 years)

1.

2.

Long Term (2 years or more)

1.

2.

5.4c   Are your institution's research, scholarship, and service activities systematically evaluated and improved?

Notes for application writing:

Zero-Based   World-Class

0	10	20	30	40	50	60	70	80	90	100

(Circle Appropriate Percentile)

Zero-Based Institution

- *No evaluation is conducted of research, scholarship, and service activities.*

- *No comparisons or benchmarking of other institutions are conducted.*

- *Institution is not concerned with improving research, scholarship, and service activities.*

World-Class Institution

- *Institution evaluates research, scholarship, and service activities by benchmarking other institutions that have been identified as being the best within these areas.*

- *Annual feedback from participants and beneficiaries is conducted for continuous process improvement.*

- *Measurement indicators have been developed to gauge the benefit that research, scholarship, and service have on the institution's key communities.*

☑ Approach   ☑ Deployment   ☐ Results

5.4c   Institution's evaluation and improvement of research, scholarship, and service activities.

+ Strengths

1.

2.

3.

- Opportunities for Improvement

1.

2.

3.

Strategic Planning Issues:

Short Term (1 to 2 years)

1.

2.

Long Term (2 years or more)

1.

2.

5.5 NOTES

5.5   Enrollment Management (20 points)

Describe how the institution manages its recruitment, admissions, and/or entry processes to ensure effective transitions for incoming students. Describe also the institution's actions and plans to improve the preparation of potential students.

AREAS TO ADDRESS

a. how the institution communicates key requirements to feeder schools, families, and prospective students to ensure proper choice and effective transition. Describe how the following are addressed: (1) equity; (2) orientation, placement, and other services; and (3) feedback to feeder schools.

b. how the institution evaluates and improves its management of interactions with feeder schools, prospective students, and families. Describe current actions and plans: (1) to assist feeder schools and families to make proper choices and to prepare students for entry; and (2) to improve selection and admissions processes based upon feedback from feeder schools, students, and families.

**5.5
PERCENT
SCORE**

 Approach

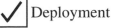 Deployment

☐ Results

5.5a   How does your institution communicate requirements to feeder schools, families, and prospective students?

Notes for application writing:

Zero-Based   World-Class

0	10	20	30	40	50	60	70	80	90	100

(Circle Appropriate Percentile)

Zero-Based Institution

- *The institution does not communicate requirements to feeder schools, families, and prospective students.*

- *Admissions requirements are not communicated clearly to feeder schools, families, and prospective students.*

- *The institution does limited recruiting and does not work with feeder and area schools.*

World-Class Institution

- *The institution has developed partnerships with key school districts to coordinate admission requirements.*

- *A simplified brochure has been produced for prospective students that details admission requirements.*

- *The institution holds semiannual workshops for guidance counselors within key school districts to communicate requirements and institutional changes.*

☑ Approach   ☑ Deployment   ☐ Results

5.5a Institution's communication of requirements to feeder schools, families, and prospective students.

+ Strengths

1.

2.

3.

- Opportunities for Improvement

1.

2.

3.

Strategic Planning Issues:

Short Term (1 to 2 years)

1.

2.

Long Term (2 years or more)

1.

2.

5.5b   Does your institution evaluate and improve its relationship with feeder schools, prospective students, and families?

Notes for application writing:

Zero-Based   World-Class

| 0 | 10 | 20 | 30 | 40 | 50 | 60 | 70 | 80 | 90 | 100 |

(Circle Appropriate Percentile)

Zero-Based Institution

- *Institution is not concerned with improving its relationship with feeder schools, prospective students, and families.*

- *Institution changes admission and assessment requirements with no plans in place to notify feeder schools.*

- *No workshops are held and very little communication to feeder schools, prospective students, and families is attempted to communicate admission requirements.*

World-Class Institution

- *Institution works closely with senior administrators within key school districts addressing admission and assessment requirements.*

- *Institution has formed a customer council to receive input from feeder schools, prospective students, and families regarding the institution's admission requirements.*

- *Annual superintendents' workshop held to communicate requirements for students of feeder and area schools.*

☑ Approach   ☑ Deployment   ☐ Results

5.5b   Institution evaluates and improves relationships with feeder schools, prospective students, and families.

+ Strengths

1.

2.

3.

Opportunities for Improvement

1.

2.

3.

Strategic Planning Issues:

Short Term (1 to 2 years)

1.

2.

Long Term (2 years or more)

1.

2.

5.6 NOTES

5.6 Business Operations Management (20 points)

Describe how the institution's key business operations are managed so that current requirements are met and operational performance is continuously improved.

AREAS TO ADDRESS

a. how the institution ensures effective management of its key business operations. For each key business operation, describe: (1) how customers are defined; (2) how key customer requirements are determined; (3) how measures and/or indicators and goals are set; and (4) how performance is monitored. For key purchasing activities, briefly describe how requirements are communicated to suppliers and how the institution determines whether or not its requirements are met by suppliers.

b. how business operations are evaluated and improved to achieve better performance, including cost, productivity, and cycle time. Describe how each of the following is used or considered: (1) feedback from customers of the processes; (2) benchmarking processes, performance, and cost; and (3) process analysis/redesign. For key purchasing activities, briefly describe the supplier improvement process.

5.6
PERCENT
SCORE

 Approach    Deployment   ☐ Results

5.6a   How does your institution ensure effective management of its business and support operations (e.g., accounting, plant and facilities management, secretarial, security, marketing, bookstores, food services, and purchasing)?

Notes for application writing:

Zero-Based   World-Class

| 0 | 10 | 20 | 30 | 40 | 50 | 60 | 70 | 80 | 90 | 100 |

(Circle Appropriate Percentile)

Zero-Based Institution

- *Employee input is not encouraged within business and support operations.*

- *Improved operational performance and cycle time reduction is not considered within the business and support operations.*

- *Customer feedback is not used for process improvement within business and support operations.*

World-Class Institution

- *Employee teams identify and flowchart all key processes within their work areas to ensure improved operational performance and cycle time.*

- *Supplier partnerships with key institutional suppliers are developed with purchasing.*

- *Self-directed work teams are deployed within business and support areas throughout the institution.*

 Approach   ☑ Deployment   ☐ Results

5.6a   Institution's management of business and support operations.

+ Strengths

1.

2.

3.

- Opportunities for Improvement

1.

2.

3.

Strategic Planning Issues:

Short Term (1 to 2 years)

1.

2.

Long Term (2 years or more)

1.

2.

5.6b   How does your institution evaluate and improve its business and support operations (e.g., cost, productivity, and cycle-time improvement)?

Notes for application writing:

Zero-Based										World-Class
0	10	20	30	40	50	60	70	80	90	100

(Circle Appropriate Percentile)

Zero-Based Institution

- *No customer surveys or customer focus groups are conducted by the institution.*

- *Benchmarking is not used to evaluate and improve business and support operations within the institution.*

- *Institution does not consistently evaluate its business operations for improved performance.*

World-Class Institution

- *Customer surveys are conducted annually.*

- *Institution developed a monthly supplier report card for all key suppliers. Suppliers are recognized for maintaining a targeted score annually.*

- *Key process benchmarks are identified within business and support operations and used to gauge improvement.*

☑ Approach   ☑ Deployment   ☐ Results

5.6b   Institution evaluates and improves its business and support operations.

+ Strengths

1.

2.

3.

- Opportunities for Improvement

1.

2.

3.

Strategic Planning Issues:

Short Term (1 to 2 years)

1.

2.

Long Term (2 years or more)

1.

2.

CHAPTER EIGHT

Category 6.0
Institution's Performance
Results

6.0 Institution's Performance Results (230 points)[11]

The Institution's Performance Results Category examines student performance and improvement, in the institution's education climate, institutional services, and improvement in performance of the institution's business operations. Also examined are performance levels relative to comparable institutions and/or appropriately selected organizations.

---

[11] Source: Quality and Operational Results Category 6.0 has been rewritten and revised for institutions of higher education and simplified based on the 1995 Malcolm Baldrige National Quality Award Education Pilot Criteria.

6.1 Student Performance Results (100 points)

Summarize results of improvement in student performance using key measures and/or indicators of such performance.

AREAS TO ADDRESS

a. current levels and trends in key measures and/or indicators of student performance.

b. for the results presented in 6.1a, demonstrate that there has been improvement in student performance.

c. for the results presented in 6.1a, show how student performance and performance trends compare with comparable institutions and or comparable student populations.

6.1
PERCENT
SCORE

☐ Approach   ☐ Deployment   ☑ Results

6.1a   Does your institution collect student performance data?

Notes for application writing:

Zero-Based   World-Class

0	10	20	30	40	50	60	70	80	90	100

(Circle Appropriate Percentile)

Zero-Based Institution

- *Institution does not collect student performance data.*

- *Student performance data are not used to gauge improvement within the institution.*

- *Student performance data are used only for marketing the institution, not for gauging improved student performance.*

World-Class Institution

- *Student performance trend data are collected within each division of the institution.*

- *Student trend data indicate that the institutions primary improvement objectives are being met.*

- *Student placement-results data over three years have been validated and indicate that student placement is a direct result of changed curriculum.*

☐ Approach   ☐ Deployment   ☑ Results

6.1a   Institution's student performance data.

+ Strengths

1.

2.

3.

- Opportunities for Improvement

1.

2.

3.

Strategic Planning Issues:

   Short Term (1 to 2 years)

    1.

    2.

   Long Term (2 years or more)

    1.

    2.

6.1b   How does your institution validate student performance data?

Notes for application writing:

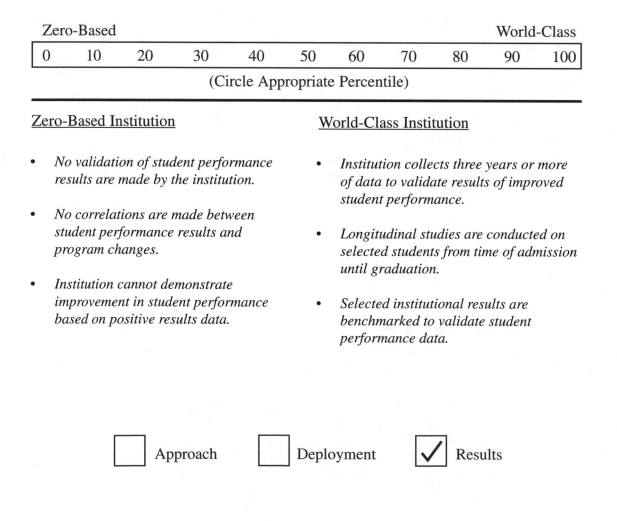

Zero-Based   World-Class

| 0 | 10 | 20 | 30 | 40 | 50 | 60 | 70 | 80 | 90 | 100 |

(Circle Appropriate Percentile)

Zero-Based Institution

- *No validation of student performance results are made by the institution.*

- *No correlations are made between student performance results and program changes.*

- *Institution cannot demonstrate improvement in student performance based on positive results data.*

World-Class Institution

- *Institution collects three years or more of data to validate results of improved student performance.*

- *Longitudinal studies are conducted on selected students from time of admission until graduation.*

- *Selected institutional results are benchmarked to validate student performance data.*

☐ Approach   ☐ Deployment   ☑ Results

6.1b   Institution's validation of student performance data.

+ Strengths

1.

2.

3.

- Opportunities for Improvement

1.

2.

3.

Strategic Planning Issues:

   Short Term (1 to 2 years)

   1.

   2.

   Long Term (2 years or more)

   1.

   2.

6.1c   Does your institution compare students performance and performance trends against other institutions?

Notes for application writing:

Zero-Based   World-Class

0	10	20	30	40	50	60	70	80	90	100

(Circle Appropriate Percentile)

Zero-Based Institution

- *Institution does no comparisons of student performance data outside the institution.*

- *Data comparisons of student performance are not considered by the institution.*

- *Student performance and performance trend data are considered confidential information by the institution.*

World-Class Institution

- *Institution has selected two student performance indicators to compare performance trends.*

- *Institution has identified a comparable institution with a similar student population to compare student performance results.*

- *Results data are compared against National Education Benchmark Clearinghouse data.*

☐ Approach   ☐ Deployment   ☑ Results

6.1c   Institution's comparisons of student performance and performance trends against other institutions.

+ Strengths

1.

2.

3.

- Opportunities for Improvement

1.

2.

3.

Strategic Planning Issues:

Short Term (1 to 2 years)

1.

2.

Long Term (2 years or more)

1.

2.

6.2 NOTES

6.2 Institution's Education Climate Improvement Results (50 points)

Summarize results of improvement in the institution's education climate using key measures and/or indicators.

AREAS TO ADDRESS

a. current levels and trends in key measures and/or indicators of institution's education climate. Graphs and tables listed should include appropriate comparative data, when available.

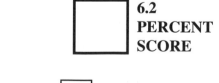

6.2
PERCENT
SCORE

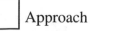

☐ Approach   ☐ Deployment   ☑ Results

6.2a   Does your institution collect data that gauge its educational climate (e.g., student drop-out rates and absenteeism, faculty absenteeism, faculty turnover, and students' institutional involvement, etc.)?

Notes for application writing:

Zero-Based   World-Class

0	10	20	30	40	50	60	70	80	90	100

(Circle Appropriate Percentile)

Zero-Based Institution

- *Institution collects no data to gauge educational climate.*

- *Faculty turnover is of no concern to the institution. Survey data are not used to help determine contributing factors.*

- *Institution's use of data are limited to grant writing and funding requests.*

World-Class Institution

- *Institution collects data on student drop-out rates within selected programs to determine critical factors that might impact learning.*

- *Student survey data results are used to improve student educational programs and support services.*

- *Faculty climate surveys are conducted annually to help determine faculty satisfaction and well-being.*

☐ Approach   ☐ Deployment   ☑ Results

6.2a   Institution's collection of data to gauge educational climate.

+ Strengths

1.

2.

3.

- Opportunities for Improvement

1.

2.

3.

Strategic Planning Issues:

Short Term (1 to 2 years)

1.

2.

Long Term (2 years or more)

1.

2.

6.3 NOTES

6.3 Research, Scholarship, and Service Results (40 points)

Summarize results of improvement in the institution's contribution to knowledge, knowledge transfer, and service.

AREAS TO ADDRESS

a. current levels and trends in key measures and/or indicators of the institution's contribution to knowledge, knowledge transfer, and service. Graphs and tables should include appropriate comparative data.

6.3 PERCENT SCORE

☐ Approach   ☐ Deployment   ☑ Results

6.3a   Does your institution collect data on research, scholarship, and service results?

Notes for application writing:

Zero-Based   World-Class

0	10	20	30	40	50	60	70	80	90	100

(Circle Appropriate Percentile)

Zero-Based Institution

- *No data base is maintained on faculty/ staff research publications.*

- *Limited data are collected on community service projects conducted by faculty/staff.*

- *No trend data are maintained on the institution's contribution to knowledge, knowledge transfer, and service.*

World-Class Institution

- *Research grants, faculty publications, and faculty service project data are compared against leading institutions.*

- *Service project data are compared against national averages within comparable institutions.*

- *Trend data are maintained on each faculty member and department regarding research grants and publications produced each year.*

☐ Approach   ☐ Deployment   ☑ Results

6.3a   Institutional data on research, scholarship, and service results.

+ Strengths

1.

2.

3.

- Opportunities for Improvement

1.

2.

3.

Strategic Planning Issues:

   Short Term (1 to 2 years)

      1.

      2.

   Long Term (2 years or more)

      1.

      2.

6.4 NOTES

6.4 Institution's Business Performance Results (40 points)

Summarize results of improvement efforts using key measures and/or indicators of institution's business operational and financial performance.

AREAS TO ADDRESS

a. current levels and trends in key measures and/or indicators of institution's business operational and financial performance. Graphs and tables should include appropriate comparative and benchmark data.

6.4 PERCENT SCORE

☐ Approach   ☐ Deployment   ☑ Results

6.4a   Does your institution collect data on business operations?

Notes for application writing:

Zero-Based   World-Class

0	10	20	30	40	50	60	70	80	90	100

(Circle Appropriate Percentile)

Zero-Based Institution

- *Limited data are maintained on business operations and financial performance within key support areas of the institution.*

- *Business support data are not maintained within the institution.*

- *Key supplier performance data are not consistently collected and used to support improved supplier performance.*

World-Class Institution

- *Cycle-time reduction data are collected within personnel department on new hire placement.*

- *Waste reduction data are maintained on several processes within the institution's physical plant department.*

- *Energy conservation data are maintained within each division throughout the institution.*

☐ Approach   ☐ Deployment   ☑ Results

6.4a   Institution's data on business operations.

+ Strengths

1.

2.

3.

- Opportunities for Improvement

1.

2.

3.

Strategic Planning Issues:

   Short Term (1 to 2 years)

   1.

   2.

   Long Term (2 years or more)

   1.

   2.

CHAPTER NINE

Category 7.0
Satisfaction of Those
Receiving Services _____

7.0 Satisfaction of Those Receiving Services (230 points)[12]

The Satisfaction of Those Receiving Services Category examines the educational institution's relationship with students, stakeholders, and other customers and its knowledge of their requirements. Also examined are the institution's methods to determine student, stakeholder, and other customer satisfaction, current needs and levels in student, stakeholder, and other customer satisfaction and retention, and these results relative to other educational institutions.

---

[12] Source: Satisfaction of Those Receiving Services Category 7.0 has been rewritten and revised for institutions of higher education and simplified based on the 1995 Malcolm Baldrige National Quality Award Education Pilot Criteria.

7.1 Current Student Needs and Expectations (40 points)

Describe how the institution develops and maintains awareness of the needs and expectations of current students and seeks to create an overall climate conducive to active learning, well-being, and satisfaction for all students.

AREAS TO ADDRESS

a. how the institution develops and maintains awareness of key general and special needs and expectations of current students. Describe: (1) how student needs and expectations are determined, aggregated, and analyzed to ensure the availability and preparation of appropriate offerings, facilities, and services; and (2) how this information is deployed to all appropriate institutional units.

b. how the institution monitors student utilization of offerings, facilities, and services to determine their influence upon satisfaction and active learning. Include how information on student segments and/or individual students is developed for purposes of engaging students in active learning.

c. how the institution evaluates and improves its processes for determining current student needs and expectations. Describe: (1) how this process utilizes information from students, faculty, staff, and other stakeholders; and (2) how this information is used throughout the institution to improve satisfaction and active learning.

7.1 PERCENT SCORE

 Approach  Deployment ☐ Results

7.1a   How does your institution determine requirements and expectations of current students and other customers (e.g., student/customer focus groups, surveys, etc.)?

Notes for application writing:

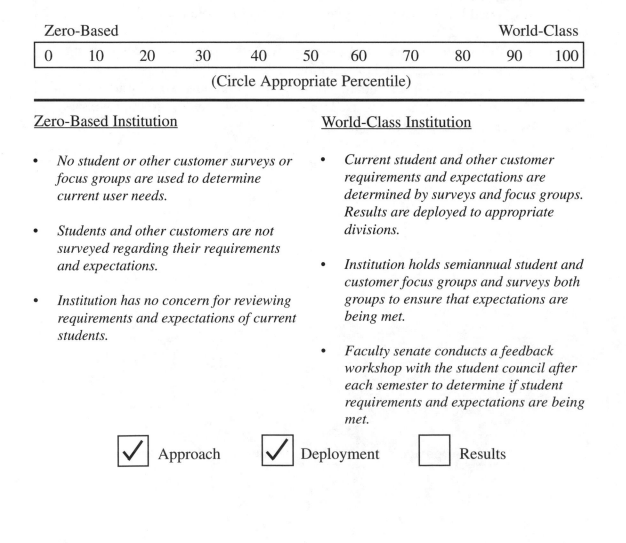

Zero-Based   World-Class

| 0 | 10 | 20 | 30 | 40 | 50 | 60 | 70 | 80 | 90 | 100 |

(Circle Appropriate Percentile)

Zero-Based Institution

- *No student or other customer surveys or focus groups are used to determine current user needs.*

- *Students and other customers are not surveyed regarding their requirements and expectations.*

- *Institution has no concern for reviewing requirements and expectations of current students.*

World-Class Institution

- *Current student and other customer requirements and expectations are determined by surveys and focus groups. Results are deployed to appropriate divisions.*

- *Institution holds semiannual student and customer focus groups and surveys both groups to ensure that expectations are being met.*

- *Faculty senate conducts a feedback workshop with the student council after each semester to determine if student requirements and expectations are being met.*

☑ Approach   ☑ Deployment   ☐ Results

7.1a   Institution determines requirements and expectations of current students and other customers.

+ Strengths

1.

2.

3.

- Opportunities for Improvement

1.

2.

3.

Strategic Planning Issues:

Short Term (1 to 2 years)

1.

2.

Long Term (2 years or more)

1.

2.

7.1b   How does your institution monitor student and other customer use of programs, offerings, facilities, and services?

Notes for application writing:

Zero-Based   World-Class

| 0 | 10 | 20 | 30 | 40 | 50 | 60 | 70 | 80 | 90 | 100 |

(Circle Appropriate Percentile)

Zero-Based Institution

- *Institution does not monitor offerings, facilities, and services.*

- *Institution has no process in place for monitoring students with similar learning styles, interests, living status (on campus vs. off campus), or other factors that promote improved active learning.*

- *The institution does not monitor how its offerings, facilities, and services impact student and other customer satisfaction and promote active learning.*

World-Class Institution

- *Institution monitors, on a semester basis, all new programs, facilities use, and new services rendered to gauge continuation or modification of the new offerings.*

- *Student and other customer evaluation cards are used to monitor all programs, facilities, and services.*

- *All programs, facilities, and services are formally assessed annually by a cross-functional team comprised of students, faculty, staff, and customers.*

☑ Approach   ☑ Deployment   ☐ Results

7.1b   Institution's monitoring of student and other customer use of program offerings, facilities, and services.

+ Strengths

1.

2.

3.

- Opportunities for Improvement

1.

2.

3.

Strategic Planning Issues:

Short Term (1 to 2 years)

1.

2.

Long Term (2 years or more)

1.

2.

7.1c   How does your institution evaluate and improve its processes for determining current student and other customer requirements and expectations?

Notes for application writing:

Zero-Based   World-Class

0	10	20	30	40	50	60	70	80	90	100

(Circle Appropriate Percentile)

Zero-Based Institution

- *Institution appears weak in evaluating current and other customer requirements and expectations.*

- *Institution does not have a process in place to determine student and other customer requirements and expectations.*

- *Institution surveys current students and customers, but does not use this data to change processes for improvement.*

World-Class Institution

- *Institution has a survey program in place to determine current student and other customer requirements and expectations.*

- *Institution uses student and other customer focus groups and the student advisory council to address current student/customer requirements and expectations.*

- *Institution uses survey and focus group data from current students and customers and incorporates changes in its offerings, facilities, and services.*

☑ Approach   ☑ Deployment   ☐ Results

7.1c   Institution evaluates and improves its determination of current student and other customer requirements and expectations.

+ Strengths

1.

2.

3.

- Opportunities for Improvement

1.

2.

3.

Strategic Planning Issues:

Short Term (1 to 2 years)

1.

2.

Long Term (2 years or more)

1.

2.

7.2 NOTES

7.2 Future Student Needs and Expectations (30 points)

Describe how the institution determines needs and expectations of future students and maintains awareness of the key factors affecting these needs and expectations.

AREAS TO ADDRESS

a. how the institution determines and anticipates changing needs and expectations for future students. Summarize: (1) demographic factors and trends that may bear upon enrollments and needs; (2) changing requirements and expectations its graduates will face; (3) changing needs and expectations resulting from national, state, or local requirements; and (4) educational alternatives available to its pool of future students. For each of these four factors, briefly describe the basis for the conclusions.

b. how the institution analyzes the information from 7.2a to develop actionable data and information for planning.

c. how the institution evaluates and improves its processes for determining emerging needs and expectations. Describe: (1) how the institution's own trend data are used to support the determination; and (2) how reports of national, state, educational, and research organizations are used.

7.2
PERCENT
SCORE

 Approach   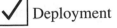 Deployment   ☐ Results

7.2a   How does your institution address future programs and services for students, other customers, and stakeholders?

Notes for application writing:

Zero-Based   World-Class

| 0 | 10 | 20 | 30 | 40 | 50 | 60 | 70 | 80 | 90 | 100 |

(Circle Appropriate Percentile)

Zero-Based Institution

- *Institution does not address future requirements and expectations of students, other customers, and stakeholders.*

- *No comparisons or benchmarking take place to help determine future program and service features for students, other customers, and stakeholders.*

- *Future programs and services are reviewed once every five years by senior institutional officers and few changes are incorporated.*

World-Class Institution

- *Cross-functional faculty, staff, and student teams undertake the task of projecting future requirements and expectations of students, other customers, and stakeholders.*

- *Student and customer-contact employees meet quarterly to determine future offerings, facilities, and services based on input from students, employers, government, and various national, state, educational and research organizations.*

- *Institution-wide suggestion program in place to receive input regarding future programs and services.*

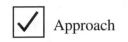 ✓ Approach   ✓ Deployment   ☐ Results

7.2a   Institution addresses future programs and services for students, other customers, and stakeholders.

+ Strengths

1.

2.

3.

- Opportunities for Improvement

1.

2.

3.

Strategic Planning Issues:

Short Term (1 to 2 years)

1.

2.

Long Term (2 years or more)

1.

2.

7.2b   Does your institution analyze future program information received from students, other customers, and stakeholders and develop it into planning and actionable data?

Notes for application writing:

Zero-Based   World-Class

0	10	20	30	40	50	60	70	80	90	100

(Circle Appropriate Percentile)

Zero-Based Institution

- *Institution does not consider future program information when developing new programs.*

- *Changing requirements and employer expectations of graduates are never considered by institution when planning.*

- *Changing needs in national, state, and local requirements are seldom considered when planning for new programs and services and modifying existing offerings.*

World-Class Institution

- *Institution incorporates all future program information when making changes in programs and services.*

- *Qualification standards, licensure requirements, and workplace skills are considered by the institution before developing new programs and services.*

- *Local factors and national trends are considered before developing new programs and modifying existing programs.*

☑ Approach   ☑ Deployment   ☐ Results

7.2b   Institution's analysis and development of future program information into planning and actionable data.

+ Strengths

1.

2.

3.

- Opportunities for Improvement

1.

2.

3.

Strategic Planning Issues:

Short Term (1 to 2 years)

1.

2.

Long Term (2 years or more)

1.

2.

7.2c How does your institution evaluate and improve its process for determining emerging needs and expectations of students, other customers, and stakeholders?

Notes for application writing:

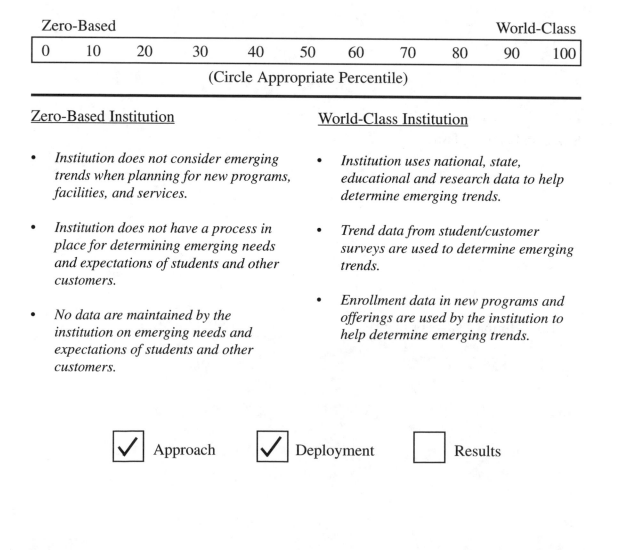

Zero-Based   World-Class

0	10	20	30	40	50	60	70	80	90	100

(Circle Appropriate Percentile)

Zero-Based Institution

- *Institution does not consider emerging trends when planning for new programs, facilities, and services.*

- *Institution does not have a process in place for determining emerging needs and expectations of students and other customers.*

- *No data are maintained by the institution on emerging needs and expectations of students and other customers.*

World-Class Institution

- *Institution uses national, state, educational and research data to help determine emerging trends.*

- *Trend data from student/customer surveys are used to determine emerging trends.*

- *Enrollment data in new programs and offerings are used by the institution to help determine emerging trends.*

☑ Approach   ☑ Deployment   ☐ Results

7.2c   Institution's determination of emerging needs and expectations.

+ Strengths

1.

2.

3.

- Opportunities for Improvement

1.

2.

3.

Strategic Planning Issues:

Short Term (1 to 2 years)

1.

2.

Long Term (2 years or more)

1.

2.

7.3 NOTES

7.3 Stakeholder Relationship Management (40 points)

Describe how the institution provides effective linkages to key stakeholders to support and enhance the institution's mission-related services and to meet stakeholder needs and expectations.

AREAS TO ADDRESS

a. how the institution creates clear bases for relationships with key stakeholders. For each stakeholder, describe: (1) key objectives of the relationship; (2) key needs of the stakeholder and how these needs are determined and kept current; and (3) key needs of the institution and how these needs are communicated to the stakeholders.

b. how the institution maintains effective stakeholder relationships. Describe: (1) how regular and special access needs are addressed; (2) how the institution follows up on its interactions with key stakeholders to determine satisfaction, progress in meeting objectives, and to resolve problems; (3) key measures and/or indicators the institution uses to monitor the effectiveness and progress of its key relationships; and (4) how the institution develops partnerships with key stakeholders to pursue common purposes.

c. how the institution evaluates and improves its relationships with key stakeholders. Describe how the evaluation/improvement process operates, including the key information and data and how they are used.

7.3
PERCENT
SCORE

 Approach   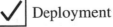 Deployment   Results

7.3a   How does your institution maintain and build relationships with key stakeholders?

Notes for application writing:

Zero-Based   World-Class

0	10	20	30	40	50	60	70	80	90	100

(Circle Appropriate Percentile)

Zero-Based Institution

- *President and other senior institutional officers are only involved with community, governmental, educational, and business leaders in a time of crisis.*

- *Institution does not systematically identify and determine individual stakeholders needs to maintain and build ongoing relationships.*

- *Key stakeholders have not been identified by the institution.*

World-Class Institution

- *Roundtable sessions are held with past graduates, employers, legislators, and key school district administrators to determine key needs of each stakeholder.*

- *Institution conducts an annual community forum with key business, government, and educational leaders to share and communicate institutional needs.*

- *Key community, business, governmental, and educational leaders meet quarterly with the president's council to share ideas and maintain and build ongoing relationships.*

☑ Approach   ☑ Deployment   ☐ Results

7.3a   Institution maintains and builds relationships with key stakeholders.

+ Strengths

1.

2.

3.

- Opportunities for Improvement

1.

2.

3.

Strategic Planning Issues:

    Short Term (1 to 2 years)

      1.

      2.

    Long Term (2 years or more)

      1.

      2.

7.3b   How does your institution maintain effective stakeholder relationships?

Notes for application writing:

Zero-Based   World-Class

0	10	20	30	40	50	60	70	80	90	100

(Circle Appropriate Percentile)

Zero-Based Institution

- *Institution does not maintain ongoing relationships with past graduates, employers, and social service organizations.*

- *Relationships with key stakeholders are only during established crisis events.*

- *No key measures or indicators are in place to monitor effectiveness and progress of stakeholder relationships.*

World-Class Institution

- *Institution has formed a partnership with key community employers to help determine program offerings for students.*

- *Institution conducts surveys of major employers to determine satisfaction with recent graduates that have been employed.*

- *Annual partnership meetings are held with key legislators to review program changes and proposed additions.*

☑ Approach   ☑ Deployment   ☐ Results

7.3b   Institution maintains stakeholder relationships.

+ Strengths

1.

2.

3.

- Opportunities for Improvement

1.

2.

3.

Strategic Planning Issues:

    Short Term (1 to 2 years)

       1.

       2.

    Long Term (2 years or more)

       1.

       2.

7.3c   How does your institution evaluate and improve relationships with key stakeholders?

Notes for application writing:

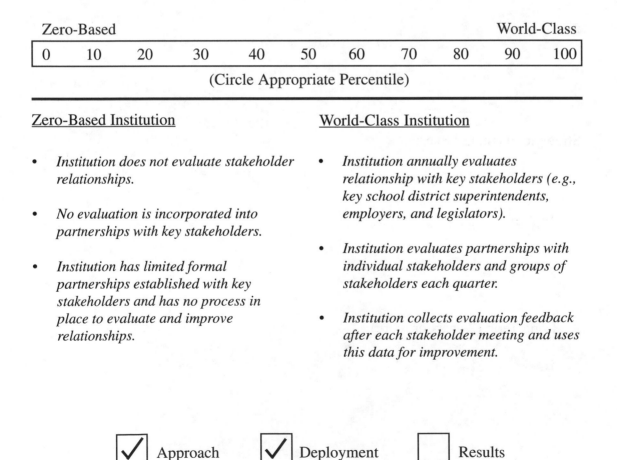

Zero-Based   World-Class

| 0 | 10 | 20 | 30 | 40 | 50 | 60 | 70 | 80 | 90 | 100 |

(Circle Appropriate Percentile)

Zero-Based Institution

- *Institution does not evaluate stakeholder relationships.*

- *No evaluation is incorporated into partnerships with key stakeholders.*

- *Institution has limited formal partnerships established with key stakeholders and has no process in place to evaluate and improve relationships.*

World-Class Institution

- *Institution annually evaluates relationship with key stakeholders (e.g., key school district superintendents, employers, and legislators).*

- *Institution evaluates partnerships with individual stakeholders and groups of stakeholders each quarter.*

- *Institution collects evaluation feedback after each stakeholder meeting and uses this data for improvement.*

☑ Approach   ☑ Deployment   ☐ Results

7.3c   Institution evaluates and improves stakeholder relationships.

+ Strengths

1.

2.

3.

- Opportunities for Improvement

1.

2.

3.

Strategic Planning Issues:

Short Term (1 to 2 years)

1.

2.

Long Term (2 years or more)

1.

2.

7.4 NOTES

7.4 Student and Stakeholder Satisfaction Determination (30 points)

Describe how the institution determines student and stakeholder satisfaction and their satisfaction relative to comparable institutions.

AREAS TO ADDRESS

a. how the institution determines the satisfaction of current and past students. Include: (1) a brief description of processes and measurement scales used; frequency of determination; and how objectivity and validity are ensured. Indicate significant differences, if any, in processes and measurement scales for different student groups; (2) how satisfaction measurements capture key information on factors that bear upon students' motivation and active learning; and (3) how student satisfaction relative to comparable institutions is determined.

b. how the institution determines the satisfaction of key stakeholders. Include: (1) a brief description of processes and measurement scales used; frequency of determination; and how objectivity and validity are ensured. Indicate significant differences, if any, in processes and measurement scales for different stakeholder groups; (2) how satisfaction measurements relate to education climate and student and stakeholder needs; and (3) how stakeholder satisfaction relative to comparable institutions is determined.

c. how the institution evaluates and improves its overall processes and measurement scales for determining student and stakeholder satisfaction. Include how dissatisfaction indicators such as gains and losses of students and complaints are used in the evaluation/improvement process. Describe also how the evaluation takes into account the effectiveness of the use of satisfaction information and data throughout the school.

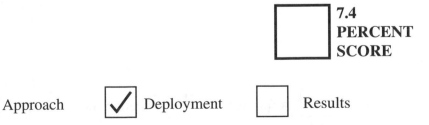

7.4
PERCENT
SCORE

☑ Approach   ☑ Deployment   ☐ Results

7.4a   How does your institution determine current and past student satisfaction levels?

Notes for application writing:

Zero-Based   World-Class

0	10	20	30	40	50	60	70	80	90	100

(Circle Appropriate Percentile)

Zero-Based Institution

- *No data exist to determine current and past student satisfaction.*

- *Institution has no concern for comparing its student satisfaction against other educational providers*

- *Institution has a high student drop-out rate, but has no process in place to determine satisfaction.*

World-Class Institution

- *Student satisfaction surveys are used to collect comparative data relative to other educational providers.*

- *Faculty and staff are encouraged to visit and benchmark other educational providers.*

- *Drop outs, complaints, and refund data are collected and compared against other educational providers who have been identified as being leading institutions.*

☑ Approach   ☑ Deployment   ☐ Results

7.4a   Institution's determination of current and past student satisfaction.

+ Strengths

1.

2.

3.

- Opportunities for Improvement

1.

2.

3.

Strategic Planning Issues:

 Short Term (1 to 2 years)

  1.

  2.

 Long Term (2 years or more)

  1.

  2.

7.4b   How does your institution determine satisfaction of key stakeholders?

Notes for application writing:

Zero-Based   World-Class

| 0 | 10 | 20 | 30 | 40 | 50 | 60 | 70 | 80 | 90 | 100 |

(Circle Appropriate Percentile)

Zero-Based Institution

- *No evidence that administration regularly reviews key stakeholder satisfaction trends and indicators and does not take deliberate actions to change processes for improvement.*

- *Institution does not recognize differences in key stakeholders.*

- *Institution is not concerned with stakeholder satisfaction issues.*

World-Class Institution

- *Institution determines key stakeholder satisfaction through its annual third-party survey.*

- *Satisfaction indicators are identified among key stakeholder groups and used to gauge satisfaction.*

- *Institutions identified as best in meeting and exceeding stakeholder satisfaction are benchmarked for comparisons.*

☑ Approach   ☑ Deployment   ☐ Results

7.4b   Institution's determination of key stakeholders satisfaction.

+ Strengths

1.

2.

3.

- Opportunities for Improvement

1.

2.

3.

Strategic Planning Issues:

    Short Term (1 to 2 years)

       1.

       2.

    Long Term (2 years or more)

       1.

       2.

7.4c How does your institution evaluate and improve its approach for determining student and stakeholder satisfaction?

Notes for application writing:

Zero-Based   World-Class

0	10	20	30	40	50	60	70	80	90	100

(Circle Appropriate Percentile)

Zero-Based Institution

- *No evidence that student/stakeholder satisfaction is compared to other leading educational providers.*

- *Institution has no concern for how competitive institutions determine student/stakeholder satisfaction.*

- *Institution does not evaluate and improve its approach for determining student/stakeholder satisfaction.*

World-Class Institution

- *Institution involves student and stakeholder contact employees in determining satisfaction.*

- *Institution uses student/stakeholder dissatisfaction data to evaluate and improve student/stakeholder relationships.*

- *Student/stakeholder focus groups are used to help institution determine student/stakeholder satisfaction relative to that of competitive institutions.*

☑ Approach   ☑ Deployment   ☐ Results

7.4c   Institution's evaluation and improvement of its approach for determining student and stakeholder satisfaction.

+ Strengths

1.

2.

3.

Opportunities for Improvement

1.

2.

3.

Strategic Planning Issues:

Short Term (1 to 2 years)

1.

2.

Long Term (2 years or more)

1.

2.

7.5 NOTES

7.5   Student and Stakeholder Satisfaction Results (50 points)

Summarize the institution's student and stakeholder satisfaction and dissatisfaction results using key measures and/or indicators of these results.

AREAS TO ADDRESS

a. current levels and trends in key measures and/or indicators of satisfaction and dissatisfaction of current and past students.

b. current levels and trends in key measures and/or indicators of satisfaction and dissatisfaction of key stakeholders.

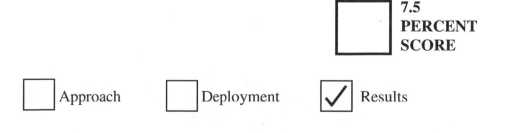

☐ 7.5 PERCENT SCORE

☐ Approach   ☐ Deployment   ☑ Results

7.5a   Does your institution collect data that measure how levels of student, other customer, and stakeholder satisfaction has changed over the last several years?

Notes for application writing:

Zero-Based										World-Class
0	10	20	30	40	50	60	70	80	90	100

(Circle Appropriate Percentile)

Zero-Based Institution

- *No data available to determine level of student satisfaction.*

- *Institution does not consider using survey trend data to determine student satisfaction.*

- *Dissatisfaction data are not trended nor used for program improvement within the institution.*

World-Class Institution

- *Institution collects trend data to measure current and past student and stakeholder satisfaction.*

- *Institution uses student trend data in its planning process.*

- *Dissatisfaction trend data are used to improve programs and schedules throughout the institution.*

☐ Approach   ☐ Deployment   ☑ Results

7.5a   Institution collects trend data to indicate levels of student and stakeholder satisfaction.

+ Strengths

1.

2.

3.

- Opportunities for Improvement

1.

2.

3.

Strategic Planning Issues:

Short Term (1 to 2 years)

1.

2.

Long Term (2 years or more)

1.

2.

7.5b   Does your institution measure key stakeholder dissatisfaction indicators such as drop outs, complaints, claims, refunds, repeat services, and litigation?

Notes for application writing:

Zero-Based   World-Class

| 0 | 10 | 20 | 30 | 40 | 50 | 60 | 70 | 80 | 90 | 100 |

(Circle Appropriate Percentile)

Zero-Based Institution

- *No documented follow-up methods, disciplines, or controls are in place to address adverse key stakeholder indicators.*

- *Key stakeholder dissatisfaction is not addressed.*

- *Stakeholder dissatisfaction data are collected and aggregated, but not incorporated into the institution's planning process.*

World-Class Institution

- *Institution leads other educational providers in reducing adverse stakeholder indicators.*

- *Adverse stakeholder indicators are shared with faculty and staff and used to improve stakeholder relationships.*

- *Stakeholder dissatisfaction data are incorporated into the institution's annual planning process.*

☐ Approach   ☐ Deployment   ☑ Results

7.5b   Institution measures current levels and trends of key stakeholder dissatisfaction.

+ Strengths

1.

2.

3.

- Opportunities for Improvement

1.

2.

3.

Strategic Planning Issues:

Short Term (1 to 2 years)

1.

2.

Long Term (2 years or more)

1.

2.

7.6 NOTES

7.6 Student and Stakeholder Satisfaction Comparison (40 points)

Compare the institution's satisfaction results with those of comparable institutions.

AREAS TO ADDRESS

a. current levels and trends in key measures and/or indicators of student satisfaction relative to comparable institutions.

b. current levels and trends in key measures and/or indicators of stakeholder
satisfaction relative to comparable institutions.

7.6
**PERCENT
SCORE**

 Approach   Deployment   Results

7.6a   Does your institution collect data that measure student satisfaction with your programs and/or services against satisfaction with comparable institution's programs/services?

Notes for application writing:

Zero-Based									World-Class	
0	10	20	30	40	50	60	70	80	90	100

(Circle Appropriate Percentile)

Zero-Based Institution

- *Institution does not collect student satisfaction data relative to comparable institutions.*

- *Institution collects anecdotal data on programs/services offered by comparable institutions.*

- *Comparison data are not considered when the institution collects student satisfaction data.*

World-Class Institution

- *Comparison data show positive trends.*

- *Institution's data versus comparable institutions data show positive trends in overall student satisfaction.*

- *Student services (e.g., financial aid, counselling, food service, and security) exhibit positive trends against comparable institutions.*

☐ Approach   ☐ Deployment   ☑ Results

7.6a   Institution's comparison of student satisfaction with programs/services relative to other institutions.

+ Strengths

1.

2.

3.

- Opportunities for Improvement

1.

2.

3.

Strategic Planning Issues:

Short Term (1 to 2 years)

1.

2.

Long Term (2 years or more)

1.

2.

7.6b   Does your institution collect data that measure stakeholder satisfaction with your programs and/or services against satisfaction with comparable institution's programs/services?

Notes for application writing:

Zero-Based										World-Class
0	10	20	30	40	50	60	70	80	90	100

(Circle Appropriate Percentile)

Zero-Based Institution

- *Institution does not measure stakeholder satisfaction.*

- *Institution's stakeholder satisfaction indicators are below those of comparable institutions.*

- *Institution does not survey and compare key stakeholders to determine satisfaction relative to competitive institutions and programs.*

World-Class Institution

- *Institution measures stakeholder satisfaction against comparable institution's programs/services.*

- *Institution's stakeholders satisfaction indicators measured against comparable institutions and rated by an independent organization reflect outstanding results.*

- *Ten outstanding service awards given by major employers have been received by the institution.*

☐ Approach   ☐ Deployment   ☑ Results

7.6b   Institution's comparison of stakeholder satisfaction with programs/services relative to other institutions.

+ Strengths

1.

2.

3.

- Opportunities for Improvement

1.

2.

3.

Strategic Planning Issues:

Short Term (1 to 2 years)

1.

2.

Long Term (2 years or more)

1.

2.

Summary of Assessment Items

Transfer all assessment item percent scores from the category worksheets.

SUMMARY OF ASSESSMENT ITEMS	Total Points Possible A	Percent Score 0-100% (10% units) B	Score (A x B) C
1.0 Leadership			
1.1 Senior Institutional Officers' Leadership	40	_____ %	_____
1.2 Leadership System and Organization	30	_____ %	_____
1.3 Public Responsibility and Citizenship	20	_____ %	_____
CATEGORY TOTAL	90		_____ (Sum C)
2.0 Information and Analysis			
2.1 Management of Information and Data	25	_____ %	_____
2.2 Comparisons and Benchmarking	15	_____ %	_____
2.3 Analysis and Use of Institution-level Data	35	_____ %	_____
CATEGORY TOTAL	75		_____ (Sum C)
3.0 Strategic and Operational Planning			
3.1 Strategy Development	45	_____ %	_____
3.2 Strategy Deployment	30	_____ %	_____
CATEGORY TOTAL	75		_____ (Sum C)
4.0 Human Resource Development and Management			
4.1 Human Resource Planning and Evaluation	30	_____ %	_____
4.2 Faculty and Staff Work Systems	30	_____ %	_____
4.3 Faculty and Staff Development	50	_____ %	_____
4.4 Faculty and Staff Well-Being and Satisfaction	40	_____ %	_____
CATEGORY TOTAL	150		_____ (Sum C)

SUMMARY OF ASSESSMENT ITEMS	Total Points Possible A	Percent Score 0-100% (10% units) B	Score (A x B) C

5.0 Educational and Business Process Management

	Total Points Possible A	Percent Score 0-100% (10% units) B	Score (A x B) C
5.1 Education Design	40	_____%	_____
5.2 Education Delivery	25	_____%	_____
5.3 Education Support Service Design and Delivery	25	_____%	_____
5.4 Research, Scholarship, and Service	20	_____%	_____
5.5 Enrollment Management	20	_____%	_____
5.6 Business Operations Management	20	_____%	_____
CATEGORY TOTAL	150		_____ (Sum C)

6.0 Institution's Performance Results

6.1 Student Performance Results	100	_____%	_____
6.2 Institution's Education Climate Improvement Results	50	_____%	_____
6.3 Research, Scholarship, and Service Results	40	_____%	_____
6.4 Institution's Business Performance Results	40	_____%	_____
CATEGORY TOTAL	230		_____ (Sum C)

7.0 Satisfaction of Those Receiving Services

7.1 Current Student Needs and Expectations	40	_____%	_____
7.2 Future Student Needs and Expectations	30	_____%	_____
7.3 Stakeholder Relationship Management	40	_____%	_____
7.4 Student and Stakeholder Satisfaction Determination	30	_____%	_____
7.5 Student and Stakeholder Satisfaction Results	50	_____%	_____
7.6 Student and Stakeholder Satisfaction Comparison	40	_____%	_____
CATEGORY TOTAL	230		_____ (Sum C)

| **TOTAL POINTS** | **1000** | | _____ |

Hierarchy of Institutional Needs

(BASED ON BALDRIGE CRITERIA FOR HIGHER EDUCATION)

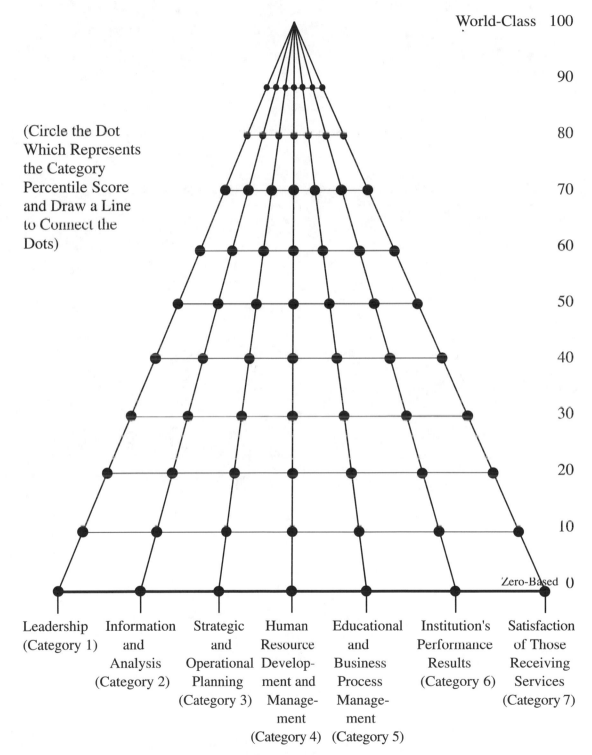

World-Class 100

90

80

(Circle the Dot
Which Represents
the Category
Percentile Score
and Draw a Line
to Connect the
Dots)

70

60

50

40

30

20

10

Zero-Based 0

Leadership
(Category 1)

Information
and
Analysis
(Category 2)

Strategic
and
Operational
Planning
(Category 3)

Human
Resource
Develop-
ment and
Manage-
ment
(Category 4)

Educational
and
Business
Process
Manage-
ment
(Category 5)

Institution's
Performance
Results
(Category 6)

Satisfaction
of Those
Receiving
Services
(Category 7)

CHAPTER TEN

Transforming Assessment Findings into Actionable Strategies for Improvement ___

The assessment of the institution is complete. Now the next step is to transform the assessment results into actionable short- and long-term strategies for institutional improvement.

The assessment team should begin this process by reviewing strengths and opportunities for improvement within the 63 areas assessed. The assessment team members will need to reach a consensus on short- and long-term strategic issues for each area. After this process is complete, the team should go back through the assessment workbook and collect item percentage scores. The assessment percentages should be shaded within each appropriate item bar graph.

INSTITUTIONAL ASSESSMENT BAR GRAPH
(Shade in assessment percentages on bar graphs from
item score boxes located throughout workbook.)

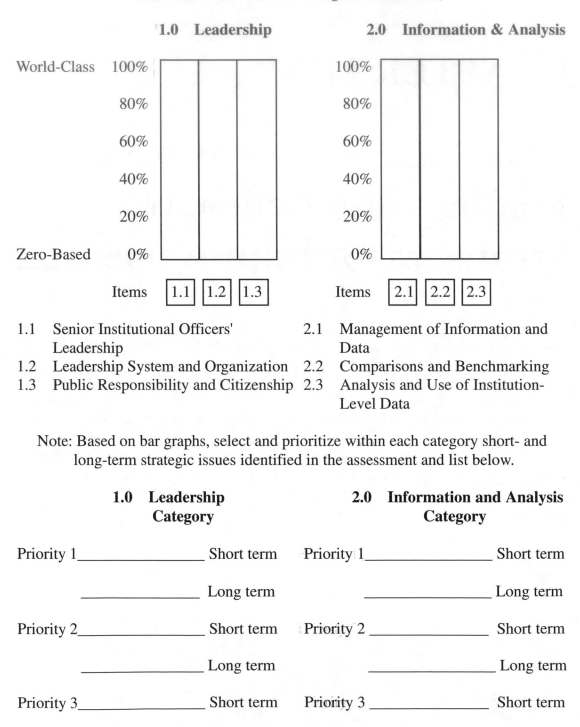

1.0	Leadership
1.1	Senior Institutional Officers' Leadership
1.2	Leadership System and Organization
1.3	Public Responsibility and Citizenship

2.0	Information & Analysis
2.1	Management of Information and Data
2.2	Comparisons and Benchmarking
2.3	Analysis and Use of Institution-Level Data

Note: Based on bar graphs, select and prioritize within each category short- and long-term strategic issues identified in the assessment and list below.

1.0   Leadership Category

Priority 1_____ Short term

_____ Long term

Priority 2_____ Short term

_____ Long term

Priority 3_____ Short term

_____ Long term

2.0   Information and Analysis Category

Priority 1_____ Short term

_____ Long term

Priority 2_____ Short term

_____ Long term

Priority 3_____ Short term

_____ Long term

INSTITUTIONAL ASSESSMENT BAR GRAPH
(Shade in assessment percentages on bar graphs from
item score boxes located throughout workbook.)

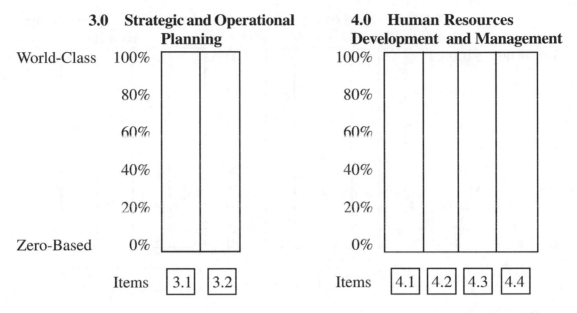

3.0 Strategic and Operational Planning

World-Class	100%
	80%
	60%
	40%
	20%
Zero-Based	0%

Items   3.1   3.2

3.1 Strategy Development
3.2 Strategy Deployment

4.0 Human Resources Development and Management

	100%
	80%
	60%
	40%
	20%
	0%

Items   4.1   4.2   4.3   4.4

4.1 Human Resource Planning and Evaluation
4.2 Faculty and Staff Work Systems
4.3 Faculty and Staff Development
4.4 Faculty and Staff Well-Being and Satisfaction

Note: Based on bar graphs, select and prioritize short- and long-term
strategic issues identified in the assessment and list below.

3.0 Strategic and Operational Planning Category

Priority 1_____ Short term

_____ Long term

Priority 2_____ Short term

_____ Long term

Priority 3_____ Short term

_____ Long term

4.0 Human Resources Development and Management Category

Priority 1 _____ Short term

_____ Long term

Priority 2 _____ Short term

_____ Long term

Priority 3 _____ Short term

_____ Long term

INSTITUTIONAL ASSESSMENT BAR GRAPH
(Shade in assessment percentages on bar graphs from
item score boxes located throughout workbook.)

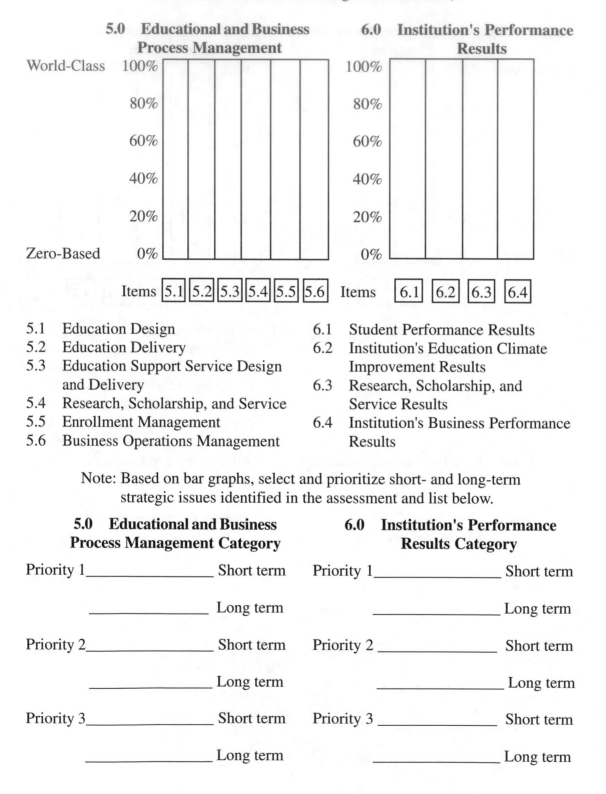

	5.0 Educational and Business Process Management	6.0 Institution's Performance Results

Items 5.1 5.2 5.3 5.4 5.5 5.6   Items 6.1 6.2 6.3 6.4

5.1   Education Design
5.2   Education Delivery
5.3   Education Support Service Design and Delivery
5.4   Research, Scholarship, and Service
5.5   Enrollment Management
5.6   Business Operations Management

6.1   Student Performance Results
6.2   Institution's Education Climate Improvement Results
6.3   Research, Scholarship, and Service Results
6.4   Institution's Business Performance Results

Note: Based on bar graphs, select and prioritize short- and long-term
strategic issues identified in the assessment and list below.

5.0 Educational and Business Process Management Category

Priority 1_____ Short term

_____ Long term

Priority 2_____ Short term

_____ Long term

Priority 3_____ Short term

_____ Long term

6.0 Institution's Performance Results Category

Priority 1_____ Short term

_____ Long term

Priority 2_____ Short term

_____ Long term

Priority 3_____ Short term

_____ Long term

INSTITUTIONAL ASSESSMENT BAR GRAPH
(Shade in assessment percentages on bar graphs from
item score boxes located throughout workbook.)

7.0   Satisfaction of Those Receiving Services

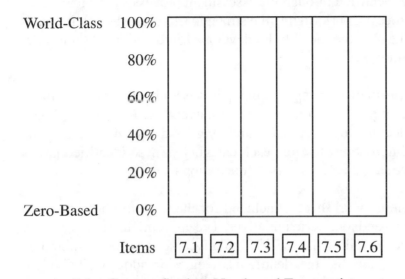

7.1   Current Student Needs and Expectations
7.2   Future Student Needs and Expectations
7.3   Stakeholder Relationship Management
7.4   Student and Stakeholder Satisfaction Determination
7.5   Student and Stakeholder Satisfaction Results
7.6   Student and Stakeholder Satisfaction Comparison

Note: Based on bar graphs, select and prioritize short- and long-term
      strategic issues identified in the assessment and list below.

7.0   Satisfaction of Those Receiving Services Category

Priority 1 _____ Short term

_____ Long term

Priority 2 _____ Short term

_____ Long term

Priority 3 _____ Short term

_____ Long term

The shaded bar graphs will help the assessment team identify specific items within each category of the institution that need improvement.

The next step for the team after all scores have been shaded in on the bar graphs is to select and prioritize short- and long-term strategic planning issues within each category that were previously identified through the assessment process by the team. The team will go through the process of prioritizing the strategic short- and long-term planning issues within each category that need to be developed into actionable improvement strategies for the institution.

After identifying and prioritizing strategic planning issues within all seven Baldrige Categories (i.e., 1.0 Leadership, 2.0 Information and Analysis, etc.), the team should reach concensus on and select the top three short- and long-term priorities offering the greatest opportunities for improvement within each category. These identified issues transform into actionable strategic initiatives (see Illustration #1).

A master strategic planning worksheet is included for the team to photocopy and use to list its prioritized short- and long-term initiatives. The appropriate category, term, and priority should be circled detailing the specific initiative. Action item(s) should be listed in respective order to accomplish the identified strategies. In addition, individual responsibilities and review and completion dates should be documented in order to transform the institution's strategic initiatives into actionable improvement. Illustration #2 details how to complete a strategic planning worksheet.

The strategic planning worksheet should be completed by the assessment overview team. The results of both the assessment and the identified strategic issues should be reported back to the institution's senior administrative leadership and ultimately integrated into the institution's annual short- and long-term strategic planning process.

ILLUSTRATION #1

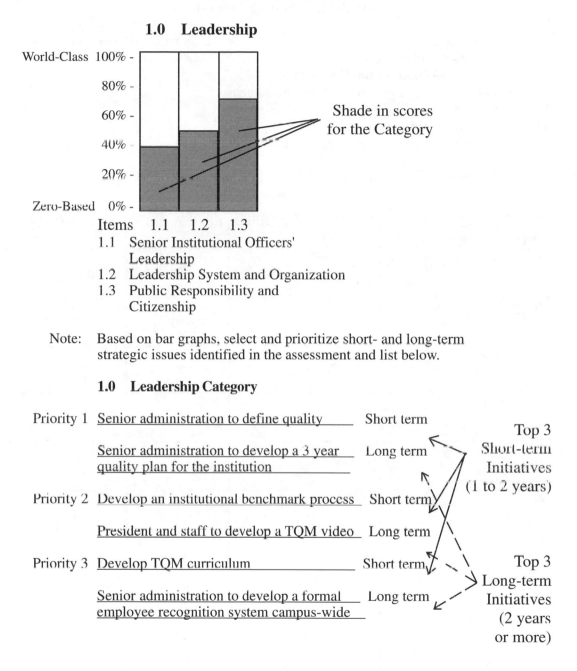

1.0   Leadership

1.1   Senior Institutional Officers' Leadership
1.2   Leadership System and Organization
1.3   Public Responsibility and Citizenship

Note: Based on bar graphs, select and prioritize short- and long-term strategic issues identified in the assessment and list below.

1.0   Leadership Category

Priority 1   Senior administration to define quality   Short term

Senior administration to develop a 3 year quality plan for the institution   Long term

Priority 2   Develop an institutional benchmark process   Short term

President and staff to develop a TQM video   Long term

Priority 3   Develop TQM curriculum   Short term

Senior administration to develop a formal employee recognition system campus-wide   Long term

Top 3 Short-term Initiatives (1 to 2 years)

Top 3 Long-term Initiatives (2 years or more)

ILLUSTRATION #2
Strategic Planning Worksheet

Category (circle one)   **Term** (circle one)

1.0   **Leadership**   **Short term: one to two years**
2.0   **Information and Analysis**   **Long term: more than two years**
3.0   **Strategic and Operational Planning**
4.0   **Human Resource Development and Management**
5.0   **Educational and Business Process Management**
6.0   **Institution's Performance Results**
7.0   **Satisfaction of Those Receiving Services**

Priority (circle one) ① 2 3   Senior Administration to Define Quality
(List Strategy Here)

ACTION ITEM(S) (Steps to accomplish strategy)	WHO IS RESPONSIBLE	REVIEW DATE	COMPLETION DATE
1. Senior staff to define quality	President	—	January 10
2. Form 2 cross-functional faculty/staff teams to review definition	Vice-President	January 30	February 28
3. Cross-functional teams to present findings to senior staff	Faculty member	March 2	March 30
4. Senior staff finalizes definition of quality	President	April 5	April 30
5. Distribute definition of quality by E-mail campus-wide	Vice-President		May 5
6.			
7.			
8.			
9.			
10.			

List action items in respective order | List individual responsibilities by name or position | List review dates | List completion dates

STRATEGIC PLANNING WORKSHEET

Category (circle one)   **Term** (circle one)
1.0   **Leadership**   **Short term: one to two years**
2.0   **Information and Analysis**   **Long term: more than two years**
3.0   **Strategic and Operational Planning**
4.0   **Human Resource Development and Management**
5.0   **Educational and Business Process Management**
6.0   **Institution's Performance Results**
7.0   **Satisfaction of Those Receiving Services**

Priority (circle one) **1 2 3** _____

ACTION ITEM(S) (Steps to accomplish strategy)	WHO IS RESPONSIBLE	REVIEW DATE	COMPLETION DATE
1.			
2.			
3.			
4.			
5.			
6.			
7.			
8.			
9.			
10.			

GLOSSARY

Institutional Assessment Glossary Based on Malcolm Baldrige National Quality Award Criteria _____

Administrative processes and support services--processes and services that may include activities and operations such as finance and accounting, software services, marketing, public relations, information services, purchasing, personnel, legal services, facilities management, research and development, secretarial and other administrative services.

Aggregated data--data that an institution has gathered together into a mass or sum so as to constitute a whole. Aggregated data are collected and used to determine an institution's achievement levels and improvement trends.

Attributes--an inherent characteristic of a product, program, or service such as cost, color, function, duration, etc.

Baldrige assessment--an institutional evaluation based on the seven categories, 28 items, and 63 areas of the Malcolm Baldrige National Quality Award Criteria.

Benchmarking--teams of employees review and visit "best-in-class" programs, services, and practices. Benchmarking can include site visits to other educational providers or noneducational organizations and telephone interviews. Benchmarking is an involved process that institutions pursue when seeking to become "world-class" in processes that they have identified as needing improvement.

Comparisons--when an institution compares its programs/services against other educational providers.

Conformance--an affirmative indicator or judgement that a program or service has met agreed-upon requirements of: (1) a student or stakeholder or (2) a relevant specification, contract, or regulation.

Consensus--collective opinion or concord; obtaining general agreement among team members.

Continuous improvement--the ongoing improvement of programs, services or processes through incremental and breakthrough improvements.

Control chart--a graph that is used by teams to determine if their work process is within prescribed limits.

Cross-functional teams--teams formed from different divisions or departments to solve or create new solutions to an institutional problem or opportunity.

Customer--the end user of all programs and services produced within an institution. Customers are both internal and external. Customers can include faculty and staff or individuals outside the institution who use programs and services provided by the institution.

Customer (internal)--a person or unit who receives product, service, or information from a fellow faculty or staff member within the same unit, department, or division—or from another unit, department, or division within the same institution of which it is a part.

Customer (external)--an outside person or organization who receives instruction, service, or information and who is not part of the institution.

Cycle time--the amount of time it takes to complete a specific work process.

Data--the collection of facts, information, or statistics.

Data analysis--the breaking apart of data to help the institution to gauge improvement.

Data management--the process by which the reliability, timeliness, and accessibility of an institution's data base is assured.

Diversity--the characteristic of a workforce which is a result of individual differences between its members. Specific differences may include gender, minority status, or individual disabilities. Workforce diversity can be a major institutional strength if the knowledge, abilities, and strengths of individual workers are recognized and respected.

Documented improvement--a process improvement that has been supported against baseline data and documented at measured intervals.

Ergonomics--the evaluation of an institution's facilities and equipment to ensure compatibility between the workforce and their work processes.

Employee involvement--involvement of faculty and staff across the institution at all levels.

Employee morale--the attitudes of faculty and staff in regard to their willingness to perform assigned tasks.

Empowerment--faculty and staff's freedom to respond to student and stakeholder demands and requests.

Flowchart--a graphic map of a work process used by teams to document the current condition of a process.

Goals and strategies--institutions develop goals and strategies for short-term (one to two years) and long-term (two years or more) desired results. Goals and strategies are usually written and distributed across the institution.

Improvement plan--a written plan that the institution has published to accomplish desired improvement results.

Institutional ethics--a published statement of values and institutional ethics which are promoted and practiced both internally and externally by the institution.

Internal customer/supplier network--an institution's employee network referred to as inside customers and suppliers.

Key indicators--key measures of performance (i.e., productivity, cycle time, cost, and other effectiveness measures).

Labor/work force--the union and nonunion employees of an institution, as well as the labor union's employees where applicable.

Measurement--the process of gauging an institution's results against their students' and customers' requirements.

Mission statement--many institutions have a published document that defines their reason for existing. The mission statement is shared with faculty, staff, students, suppliers, customers, and the community.

Partnering--the establishment of a long-term relationship between two parties characterized by teamwork and mutual trust.

Performance data--results of improvements in program and service production and delivery processes.

Performance standard--a goal against which actual performance is measured.

Plan--institutions have a strategic plan in place that is published and shared throughout the institution. Many institutions beginning their quality improvement process have a separate quality plan.

Portability--techniques and processes practiced by various colleges and universities that are applicable and can be transferred to other institutions.

Process--a series of steps linked together to provide a program or service for students and stakeholders.

Process control--a control device to detect and remove causes of variation to a defined process.

Process management--an institution's maintenance of defined processes to ensure that both quality and performance are continuously improved.

Productivity improvement--measured reduction in an institution's key operational processes.

Problem-solving tools--tools used by teams to solve process problems (i.e., flowcharts, Pareto analysis, histograms, control charts, cause-and-effect diagrams, and matrix diagrams).

Problem-solving teams--faculty and staff that form cross-functional teams, work-group teams, departmental teams, or project-focused teams that assess and analyze problems and are empowered by senior institutional officers to solve them.

Public responsibility--relates to an institution's impact or possible impact on the community and public in general with its programs, services, and operations. They include ethics, environment, health care, community services, and safety as they relate to the public.

Quality--conforming to end-users' requirements. End users may include students, faculty, or staff.

Quality assessment--an assessment of an institution's approach to and implementation of a continuous quality improvement process.

Quality control--the operational techniques and activities used to ensure that quality standards are met.

Quality results--an institution's achievement levels and improvement trends.

Root cause analysis--identifying the original cause or reason for a problem or process upset within work areas, registration, support, business and administrative areas, etc. The root cause of a condition is that cause which, if eliminated, guarantees the condition will not reoccur.

Safe work practices--an institution's promotion of safety on the worksite for employees.

Strategic plan--a detailed plan of action that an institution develops by establishing and defining measurable goals to achieve continuous quality improvement within an institution. A strategic plan can be broken into short term (one to two years) and long term (two years or more).

Senior institutional officers--refers to the institution's highest ranking officials and those reporting directly to those officials.

Stakeholders--include employees, other institutions, communities, social service organizations, legislators, etc. Key stakeholders might also be groups of stakeholders or organizations of stakeholders.

Statistical process control (SPC)--statistical technique for measuring and analyzing process variations.

Strategic planning process--addresses in detail how the institution will pursue leadership by providing superior quality programs and services and by improving the effectiveness of all operations throughout the institution.

Student/stakeholder contact employee--an employee who has direct interface with students and other stakeholders, in person, via telephone, or other means.

Supplier--an individual or group, either internal to the institution or external, that provides input.

Supplier certification program--a formal supplier program that an institution uses to help improve supplier quality. Many institutions partner with critical suppliers and establish a relationship of trust and measurable results.

Supplier partnership--many institutions establish a preferred supplier program that is based on a trust relationship with measurable results. Supplier partnerships are usually a prelude to a more formalized supplier certification program.

Survey process--an institution's survey process can include student and stakeholder, faculty and staff surveys. Survey processes help an institution to focus on satisfaction issues.

System--a set of well-defined and well-designed processes for meeting the institution's quality and performance requirements.

Targets--refers to desired goals that institutions have in their strategic planning process.

Third party survey--a survey conducted by a resource outside the institution.

Total quality management (TQM)--a management philosophy that focuses on continuous quality improvement throughout an institution.

User friendly--a process that is understandable to all levels of a workforce within an institution. A user-friendly process can be understood because it is written in simpler, more understandable language.

Values statement--a published document that describes an institution's beliefs. This values statement is usually shared with faculty, staff, students, customers, suppliers, and the community.

Vision statement--many institutions have a published document that defines their direction for the next five to ten years. The vision statement is shared with both internal and external groups.

World-class institution--an institution that produces excellent results in major areas with a sound quality management approach. This organization is totally integrated with a systematic prevention-based process that is continuously refined through evaluations and improvement cycles.

Zero-based institution--an institution that has no quality system in place and is anecdotal in its implementation of a sound, systematic, effective, and quality management-based approach that is fully integrated and implemented across the institution.

APPENDIX A
Quick and Easy Institutional Assessment ___

This abbreviated assessment can be used to help determine to what extent an institution has approached and deployed total quality management (TQM) throughout its organization. A scoring analysis is provided at the end to help determine if a more thorough assessment needs to be conducted.

This quick and easy assessment can be used to measure one's own institution or to benchmark other institutions' TQM progress.

1.0   LEADERSHIP

1. Do senior institutional officers get involved in the institution's quality efforts and focus on teaching and learning?

CIRCLE ONE

Yes--Somewhat--No

2. Do senior institutional officers communicate the institution's quality values to the community?

Yes--Somewhat--No

3. Do senior institutional officers communicate the institution's student and other customer orientation and quality values to all faculty and staff?

Yes--Somewhat--No

4. Is leadership effectiveness and personal involvement evaluated within the institution?

Yes--Somewhat--No

5. Do senior institutional officers hold everyone accountable for quality and do they have specific measures and guidelines based on their level, function, and position?

Yes--Somewhat--No

6. Do senior institutional officers ensure that the various functions within the institution are structured for effective and efficient student and stakeholder service?

Yes--Somewhat--No

7. Do senior institutional officers encourage faculty and staff to have regularly scheduled, frequent meetings during which quality of work (reduction of errors) are reviewed against the institution's plans and goals?

Yes--Somewhat--No

8. Do senior institutional officers do anything to evaluate the awareness and integration of quality values at all levels of the institution?

Yes--Somewhat--No

9. Do senior institutional officers integrate business ethics, public health and safety, environmental protection, and waste management into their work practices?

Yes--Somewhat--No

10. Do senior institutional officers encourage faculty and staff to spend time giving speeches, tours, and workshops to promote a concept of excellence to outside institutions?

Yes--Somewhat--No

Yes	Somewhat	No
10 pts.	5 pts.	0 pts.

Maximum points possible - 100   **Total Points =** _____

2.0 INFORMATION AND ANALYSIS

1. Within the institution, are data measured that all faculty and staff can understand and will that data help them provide better service to students and stakeholders?

   CIRCLE ONE:

   Yes--Somewhat--No

2. Are valid data disseminated to faculty and staff on a timely basis?

   Yes--Somewhat--No

3. Does the institution evaluate and improve the scope and quality of the data collection?

   Yes--Somewhat--No

4. Does the institution benchmark other organizations or educational institutions?

   Yes--Somewhat--No

5. Does the institution review different sources of competitive and benchmark data?

   Yes--Somewhat--No

6. Does the institution use competitive and benchmark data to encourage new ideas?

   Yes--Somewhat--No

7. Does the institution evaluate the scope and validity of comparative and benchmark data?

   Yes--Somewhat--No

8. Does the institution systematically analyze all data to identify student and other customer trends, problems, and opportunities for improvement?

   Yes--Somewhat--No

9. Does the institution collect key cost, financial, and market data and translate them into actionable information for faculty and staff to use to improve student and stakeholder service and internal performance?

   Yes--Somewhat--No

10. Does the institution evaluate and improve comparison and benchmark data received on other educational providers?

    Yes--Somewhat--No

Yes	Somewhat	No
10 pts.	5 pts.	0 pts.

Maximum points possible - 100   **Total Points = _____**

3.0   STRATEGIC AND OPERATIONAL PLANNING

1. Is the institution's overall planning process integrated with individual and institutional planning and goal setting?

CIRCLE ONE:

Yes--Somewhat--No

2. Is the institution's overall quality planning process deployed to faculty, staff, and students?

Yes--Somewhat--No

3. Is the institution's strategic plan reviewed on a continuous basis (i.e., monthly) by various levels of faculty and staff and translated into individual performance plans?

Yes--Somewhat--No

4. Does the institution have major quality improvement goals and strategies?

Yes--Somewhat--No

5. Does the institution document and share short-term (annual) goals with faculty and staff?

Yes--Somewhat--No

6. Does the institution document and share long-term goals with faculty and staff?

Yes--Somewhat--No

7. Does the institution involve faculty and staff in the strategic planning process?

Yes--Somewhat--No

8. Does the institution have a written mission statement that is shared with all faculty and staff?

Yes--Somewhat--No

9. Does a majority of faculty and staff understand the institution's mission?

Yes--Somewhat--No

10. Does the institution encourage faculty and staff to develop individual work plans that are related to the institution's strategic plans?

Yes--Somewhat--No

Yes	Somewhat	No
10 pts.	5 pts.	0 pts.

Maximum points possible - 100   **Total Points = _____**

4.0   HUMAN RESOURCE DEVELOPMENT AND MANAGEMENT

1. Is the institution's human resource plan driven by the quality goals outlined in the strategic plan? (i.e., training, development, hiring, faculty and staff involvement, empowerment, and recognition)

   <u>**CIRCLE ONE:**</u>

   Yes--Somewhat--No

2. Does the institution use faculty and staff-related data to improve human resource management? (i.e., faculty/staff selection process, quality of training, faculty/staff development)

   Yes--Somewhat--No

3. Does the institution give all faculty and staff the authority or autonomy to solve problems and make decisions within their areas of responsibility?

   Yes--Somewhat--No

4. Does the institution evaluate and measure the extent and effectiveness of efforts to increase involvement, empowerment, and innovation?

   Yes--Somewhat--No

5. Does the institution conduct a systematic needs assessment to determine the specific educational needs of different levels of faculty and staff?

   Yes--Somewhat--No

6. Does the institution employ methods and indicators to ensure that clear improvements in both faculty and staff behavior and quality improvement in their work areas are being demonstrated through improved education and training interventions?

   Yes--Somewhat--No

7. Does the institution's faculty and staff recognition and reward system support the institution's quality improvement initiatives?

   Yes--Somewhat--No

8. Does the institution encourage faculty and staff teams to constantly work on projects to improve safety, health, ergonomics, morale, and job satisfaction?

   Yes--Somewhat--No

9. Are faculty and staff encouraged to transfer to different positions and areas within the institution?

   Yes--Somewhat--No

10. Does the institution offer special services for faculty and staff?

    Yes--Somewhat--No

<u>Yes</u>	<u>Somewhat</u>	<u>No</u>
10 pts.	**5 pts.**	**0 pts.**

Maximum points possible - 100   **Total Points =** _____

5.0   EDUCATIONAL AND BUSINESS PROCESS MANAGEMENT

		CIRCLE ONE:
1.	Does the institution employ a systematic approach to gather information about student and stakeholder's requirements and desires, and then translate that information into improved program or service characteristics and standards?	Yes--Somewhat--No
2.	Does the institution have a process it uses to design and test new programs and services?	Yes--Somewhat--No
3.	Does the institution systematically evaluate and shorten design time and processes for new programs or services?	Yes--Somewhat--No
4.	Does the institution control the processes used to produce and deliver their programs and services?	Yes--Somewhat--No
5.	Does the institution promote a systematic method for analyzing the causes of process upsets?	Yes--Somewhat--No
6.	Does the institution implement a systematic, planned, and structured evaluation process that verifies predicted and consistent future results?	Yes--Somewhat--No
7.	Does the institution integrate process improvement into daily work?	Yes--Somewhat--No
8.	Does the institution handle quality control of daily processes and administrative support services?	Yes--Somewhat--No
9.	Does the institution identify opportunities for continuous improvement?	Yes--Somewhat--No
10.	Does the institution communicate specific quality requirements to major suppliers?	Yes--Somewhat--No

Yes	Somewhat	No
10 pts.	5 pts.	0 pts.

Maximum points possible - 100   **Total Points = _____**

6.0   INSTITUTIONAL PERFORMANCE RESULTS

CIRCLE ONE:

1. Does the institution have data that are related to quality improvement of student performance results and programs and services?

   Yes--Somewhat--No

2. Does the institution compare quality results against other educational providers?

   Yes--Somewhat--No

3. Does the institution collect data that measure operational performance?

   Yes--Somewhat--No

4. Does the institution compare data with that of key benchmarks and other educational providers?

   Yes--Somewhat--No

5. Does the institution have data related to quality improvement within their processes, operations, and administrative support services?

   Yes--Somewhat--No

6. Does the institution's data comparisons demonstrate that the institution is better than other educational providers within the community?

   Yes--Somewhat--No

7. Does the institution track research, scholarship, and service results?

   Yes--Somewhat--No

8. Does the institution compare major suppliers' quality to that of other educational providers?

   Yes--Somewhat--No

9. Does the institution share data with faculty and staff?

   Yes--Somewhat--No

10. Does the institution involve faculty and staff in data collection?

    Yes--Somewhat--No

Yes	Somewhat	No
10 pts.	5 pts.	0 pts.

Maximum points possible - 100   **Total Points = _____**

7.0   SATISFACTION OF THOSE RECEIVING SERVICES

1. Does the institution determine fulfillment of basic student and stakeholder needs through surveys?

   <u>CIRCLE ONE:</u>
   Yes--Somewhat--No

2. Does the institution ensure that students and stakeholders have easy access to comment on the institution's programs or services?

   Yes--Somewhat--No

3. Is the institution's survey process frequent, thorough, and objective?

   Yes--Somewhat--No

4. Does the institution develop student and stakeholder contact personnel?

   Yes--Somewhat--No

5. Does the institution analyze and use student and stakeholder-related data to develop plans and policies and allocate resources?

   Yes--Somewhat--No

6. Does the institution ensure that faculty and staff who have contact with students and stakeholders are given the latest state-of-the-art tools and technology that the institution can afford?

   Yes--Somewhat--No

7. Does the institution evaluate its performance in managing relationships with students and stakeholders?

   Yes--Somewhat--No

8. Does the institution promote trust and confidence in its services and relationships?

   Yes--Somewhat--No

9. Does the institution have data that support a trend of continuous improvement in its commitments to students and stakeholders?

   Yes--Somewhat--No

10. Does the institution evaluate and improve its student's and stakeholder's future commitments in providing better quality programs and services?

    Yes--Somewhat--No

<u>Yes</u>	<u>Somewhat</u>	<u>No</u>
10 pts.	5 pts.	0 pts.

Maximum points possible - 100   **Total Points =** _____

INSTITUTIONAL ASSESSMENT SCORE
ANALYSIS

500-700   **WORLD-CLASS**
Institution has an excellent total quality
management (TQM) process in place.
Institution should serve as a model for
other educational providers.

250-499   **QUALITY PROGRESS**
Institution has a good TQM process in
place with opportunities for improvement.

---

249 and Below   **ZERO-BASED**
Institution needs improvement in its TQM
systems. An institution-wide assessment
needs to be conducted.

APPENDIX B

Leading Institution Program/Project Benchmark Assessment Guide and Score Sheet ─────────

Benchmarking "best practices" of leading educational institutions can provide information for improving existing programs and projects. Many institutions are learning how to improve their own programs and projects by comparing them against other leading institutions and incorporating the findings into strategic improvements. This Benchmark Assessment Guide and Score Sheet can be used by a benchmark team to review "best-in-class" programs and projects within an institution or the institution as a whole. The scoring profile at the end can be used for overall scoring of the program/project or institution benchmarked. Before proceeding with a benchmarking project, the team should learn the principles of effective benchmarking (see Appendix C for recommended sources of information).

- ─────────────────────
  Institution Name

- ─────────────────────
  Title of Program/Project

- ─────────────────────
  Date(s) of Benchmark

251

KEY INSTITUTION
PROGRAM/PROJECT BUSINESS FACTORS
(List Unique Aspects of the Program/Project.)

1.

2.

3.

4.

5.

6.

7.

8.

9.

10.

11.

1.0 Senior Institutional Officers' Leadership (90 pts.)

The *Leadership* category examines senior institutional officers' *personal* leadership and involvement in creating and sustaining a focus on students and customers, developing clear and visible quality values. Also examined is how the quality values are integrated into the institution's management system, including how the institution addresses its public responsibilities and institutional citizenship.

CATEGORY 1.0 AREAS TO ADDRESS

- Do senior institutional officers get involved in the institution's quality efforts?
- Do senior institutional officers communicate the institution's quality values to the community?
- Do senior institutional officers communicate the institution's student and other customer orientation and quality values to all faculty and staff?
- Is leadership effectiveness and personal involvement evaluated within the institution?
- Do senior institutional officers hold everyone accountable for quality and do they have specific measures and guidelines based on their level, function, and position?
- Do senior institutional officers ensure that the various functions within the institution are structured for effective and efficient student and customer service?
- Do senior institutional officers encourage faculty and staff to have regularly scheduled, frequent meetings during which quality of work (reduction of errors) are reviewed against the institution's plans or goals?
- Do senior institutional officers do anything to evaluate the awareness and integration of quality values at all levels of the institution?
- Do senior institutional officers integrate business ethics, public health and safety, environmental protection, and waste management into their work practices?
- Do senior institutional officers encourage faculty and staff to spend time giving speeches, tours, and workshops to promote quality to outside institutions?

PERCENT SCORE

(+) STRENGTHS:

(-) AREAS FOR IMPROVEMENT:

BEST PRACTICES IDENTIFIED FROM THE BENCHMARK VISIT:

1.

2.

3.

2.0 Information and Analysis (75 pts.)

The *Information and Analysis* category examines the scope, validity, use, and management of data and information to drive excellence and improve overall performance compared to leading institutions.

CATEGORY 2.0 AREAS TO ADDRESS

- Within the institution are data measured that all faculty and staff can understand and will that data help provide better service to students and stakeholders?
- Are valid data disseminated to faculty and staff on a timely basis?
- Does the institution evaluate and improve the scope and quality of the data collection?
- Does the institution benchmark other organizations or educational institutions?
- Does the institution review different sources of competitive and benchmark data?
- Does the institution use competitive and benchmark data to encourage new ideas?
- Does the institution evaluate the scope and validity of comparative and benchmark data?
- Does the institution systematically analyze all data to identify student and other customer trends, problems, and opportunities for improvement?
- Does the institution collect key cost, financial, and market data and translate them into actionable information for faculty and staff to use to improve student and stakeholder service and internal performance?
- Does the institution evaluate and improve comparison and benchmark data received on other educational providers?

PERCENT SCORE

(+) STRENGTHS:

(-) AREAS FOR IMPROVEMENT:

BEST PRACTICES IDENTIFIED FROM THE BENCHMARK VISIT:

1.

2.

3.

3.0 Strategic and Operational Planning (75 pts.)

The *Strategic and Operational Planning* category examines the educational institution's planning process and how all key quality and operational performance requirements are integrated into overall institutional planning. Also examined are the institution's short-term and long-term plans and how plan requirements are de-ployed to all units.

**CATEGORY 3.0
AREAS TO ADDRESS**

- Is the institution's overall planning process integrated with individual and institutional planning and goal setting?
- Is the institution's overall quality planning process deployed to faculty, staff, and students?
- Is the institution's strategic plan reviewed on a continuous basis (i.e. , monthly) by various levels of faculty and staff and translated into individual performance plans?
- Does the institution have major quality improvement goals and strategies?
- Does the institution document and share short-term (annual) goals with faculty and staff?
- Does the institution document and share long-term goals with faculty and staff?
- Does the institution involve faculty and staff in the strategic planning process?
- Does the institution have a written mission statement that is shared with all faculty and staff?
- Does a majority of the faculty and staff understand the institution's mission?
- Does the institution encourage faculty and staff to develop individual work plans that are related to the institution's mission statement?

PERCENT SCORE

(+) STRENGTHS:

(-) AREAS FOR IMPROVEMENT:

BEST PRACTICES IDENTIFIED FROM THE BENCHMARK VISIT:

1.

2.

3.

4.0 Human Resource Development and Management (150 pts.)

The *Human Resource Development and Management* category examines the key elements of how the work force is enabled to develop its full potential to pursue the institution's quality and operational performance objectives. Also examined are the institution's efforts to build and maintain an environment for quality excellence conducive to full participation and personal and organizational growth.

CATEGORY 4.0 AREAS TO ADDRESS

- Is the institution's human resource plan driven by the quality goals outlined in the strategic plan? (i.e., training, development, hiring, faculty and staff involvement, empowerment, and recognition)
- Does the institution use faculty and staff-related data to improve human resource management? (i.e., faculty/staff selection process, quality of training, faculty/staff development)
- Does the institution give all faculty and staff the authority or autonomy to solve problems and make decisions within their areas of responsibility?
- Does the institution evaluate and measure the extent and effectiveness of efforts to increase involvement, empowerment, and innovation?
- Does the institution conduct a systematic needs assessment to determine the specific educational needs of different levels of faculty and staff?
- Does the institution employ methods and indicators to ensure that clear improvements in both faculty and staff behavior and quality improvement in their work areas are being demonstrated through improved education and training interventions?
- Does the institution's faculty and staff recognition and reward system support the institution's quality improvement initiatives?
- Does the institution encourage faculty and staff teams to constantly work on projects to improve safety, health, ergonomics, morale, and job satisfaction?
- Are faculty and staff encouraged to transfer to different positions and areas within the institution?
- Does the institution offer special services for faculty and staff?

PERCENT SCORE

(+) STRENGTHS:

(-) AREAS FOR IMPROVEMENT:

BEST PRACTICES IDENTIFIED FROM THE BENCHMARK VISIT:

1.

2.

3.

5.0 Educational and Business Process Management (150 pts.)

The *Educational and Business Process Management* category examines the systematic processes used by the educational institution to pursue ever-higher quality and institutional performance. Examined are the key elements of process management, including the development of programs and services, management of process quality for all work units and suppliers, continuous quality improvement, and quality assessment.

CATEGORY 5.0 AREAS TO ADDRESS

- Does the institution employ a systematic approach to gather information about student and stakeholder's requirements and desires, and then translate that information into improved program or service characteristics and standards?
- Does the institution have a process it uses to design and test new programs and services?
- Does the institution systematically evaluate and shorten design time and processes for new programs or services?
- Does the institution control the processes used to produce and deliver the programs and services?
- Does the institution promote a systematic method for analyzing the causes of process upsets?
- Does the institution implement a systematic, planned, and structured evaluation process that verifies predicted and consistent future results?
- Does the institution integrate process improvement into daily work?
- Does the institution handle quality control of daily processes and administrative support services?
- Does the institution identify opportunities for continuous improvement?
- Does the institution communicate specific quality requirements to major suppliers?

PERCENT SCORE

[ ]

(+) STRENGTHS:

(-) AREAS FOR IMPROVEMENT:

BEST PRACTICES IDENTIFIED FROM THE BENCHMARK VISIT:

1.

2.

3.

**6.0 Institution's
Performance Results
(230 pts.)**

The *Institution's Performance Results* category examines the institution's achievement levels and improvement trends in quality, institutional operational performance, and supplier quality. Also examined are current quality and operational performance levels relative to those of competitive educational providers.

CATEGORY 6.0
AREAS TO ADDRESS

- Does the institution have data that are related to quality improvement of student performance results and programs and services?
- Does the institution compare quality results against other educational providers?
- Does the institution collect data that measure operational performance?
- Does the institution compare data with those of key benchmarks and other educational providers?
- Does the institution have data related to quality improvement within the processes, operations, and administrative support services?
- Does the institution's data comparisons demonstrate that the institution is better than other educational providers within your community?
- Does the institution track research, scholarship, and service results?
- Does the institution compare major suppliers' quality to that of other educational providers?
- Does the institution share data with faculty and staff?
- Does the institution involve faculty and staff in data collection?

**PERCENT
SCORE**

(+) STRENGTHS:

(-) AREAS FOR IMPROVEMENT:

BEST PRACTICES IDENTIFIED FROM THE BENCHMARK VISIT:

1.

2.

3.

**7.0 Satisfaction of Those
Receiving Services
(230 pts.)**

The *Satisfaction of Those
Receiving Services* category
examines the educational
institution's relationships with
students and other customers,
and its knowledge of their
requirements. Also examined
are the institution's methods to
determine student and other
customer satisfaction, current
trends and levels in student
and other customer satis-
faction and retention, and
these results relative to other
educational institutions.

**CATEGORY 7.0
AREAS TO ADDRESS**

- Does the institution determine fulfillment of basic student and stakeholder needs through surveys?
- Does the institution ensure that students and stakeholders have easy access to comment on the institution's programs or services?
- Is the institution's survey process frequent, thorough, and objective?
- Does the institution develop student and stakeholder contact personnel?
- Does the institution analyze and use student and stakeholder-related data to develop plans and policies and allocate resources?
- Does the institution ensure that faculty and staff who have contact with students and stakeholders are given the latest state-of-the-art tools and technology that the institution can afford?
- Does the institution evaluate its performance in managing relationships with students and stakeholders?
- Does the institution promote trust and confidence in its services and relationships?
- Does the institution have data that support a trend of continuous improvements in its commitments to students and stakeholders?
- Does the institution evaluate and improve its student's and stakeholder's future commitments in providing better quality programs and services?

**PERCENT
SCORE**

(+) STRENGTHS:

(-) AREAS FOR IMPROVEMENT:

BEST PRACTICES IDENTIFIED FROM THE BENCHMARK VISIT:

1.

2.

3.

SCORING PROFILE BASED ON MALCOLM BALDRIGE
NATIONAL QUALITY AWARD CRITERIA OF THE INSTITUTION VISITED

Institution _____

SUMMARY OF EXAMINATION CATEGORIES	Total Points Possible A	Percent Score 0-100% (10% Units) B	Score (A x B) C
1.0 Leadership	90	_____ %	_____
2.0 Information and Analysis	75	_____ %	_____
3.0 Strategic and Operational Planning	75	_____ %	_____
4.0 Human Resource Development and Management	150	_____ %	_____
5.0 Educational and Business Process Management	150	_____ %	_____
6.0 Institution's Performance Results	230	_____ %	_____
7.0 Satisfaction of Those Receiving Services	230	_____ %	_____
GRAND TOTAL	1000		_____ D

Note: Baldrige Category scoring profiles presented on pages 14 to 23 of this workbook.

INSTITUTIONAL QUALITY LEVEL

(Please check appropriate quality level of institution benchmarked.)

☐ **Quality focused project/program**
Projects/programs are in place that are enhancing continuous improvement and total quality management (TQM) within the institution.

☐ **Institution focused on service quality**
The institution is applying quality principles organization-wide to its projects, programs, and processes.

☐ **World-class quality institution**
The institution is deploying quality principles in its projects, programs, and processes organization-wide and has measurable results.

APPENDIX C

Reference List for
Added Reading _____

Brown, Mark Graham. *Baldrige Award Winning Quality*, 5th Edition. New York: Quality Resources, 1995.

Camp, Robert C. *Benchmarking: The Search for Industry Best Practices that Lead to Superior Performance*. White Plains, NY: Quality Resources, 1989.

Fisher, Donald C., Julie E. Horine, Tricia H. Carlisle, and Stephen D. Williford. *Demystifying Baldrige*. New York. The Lincoln-Bradley Publishing Group, 1993.

Garvin, David. "How the Baldrige Award Really Works," Harvard Business Review, November/December, 1991, pp 80-95.

Lewis, Ralph G. and Douglas Smith. *Total Quality in Higher Education*. Delray Beach, FL: St. Lucie Press, 1994.

Malcolm Baldrige National Quality Award Educational Pilot Criteria 1995. Gaithersburg, MD: National Institute of Standards and Technology, 1995.

Malcolm Baldrige National Quality Award 1995 Midstate University Case Study, January 1995, Gaithersburg, MD: National Institute of Standards and Technology, 1995.

Rinehart, Gary. *Quality Education*. Milwaukee, WI: ASQC Quality Press, 1993.

APPENDIX D
Interviewing Hints and Tips _____

DO'S

- Be positive when asking questions.
- Allow participants time to formulate answers.
- Make sure questions are understood.
- Reword questions to aid understanding.
- Encourage all participants to answer questions.
- Appear to be interested in all respondents' answers.
- Thank participants for their time.

DONT'S

- Do not ask questions beyond what the criteria is asking.
- Never read more into the answer than is intended by the question.
- Do not ask rhetorical questions.
- Do not disagree with answers.
- Never be repetitious when asking questions.
- Do not make loaded statements when asking questions.
- Do not allow one participant to monopolize all answers.

APPENDIX E

How to Order Copies of the Education Pilot Criteria _____

The *Criteria* and the *Application Forms and Instructions* are two separate documents.

Individual Orders:

Individual copies of either document can be obtained free of charge from:

Malcolm Baldrige National Quality Award
National Institute of Standards and Technology
Route 270 and Quince Orchard Road
Administration Building, Room A537
Gaithersburg, MD 20899-0001
Telephone: 301-975-2036
Telefax: 301-948-3716